understanding marriage

understanding marriage

making it work,
or knowing
when to leave

richard taylor

Prometheus Books
59 John Glenn Drive
Amherst, New York 14228-2197

Published 2004 by Prometheus Books

Inquiries should be addressed to
Prometheus Books
59 John Glenn Drive
Amherst, New York 14228–2197
VOICE: 716–691–0133, ext. 207
FAX: 716–564–2711
WWW.PROMETHEUSBOOKS.COM

08 07 06 05 04   5 4 3 2 1

Library of Congress Cataloging-in-Publication Data

Taylor, Richard, 1919–2003.
    Understanding marriage : making it work, or knowing when to leave /
Richard Taylor.
        p. cm.
    Includes bibliographical references.
    Contents: Marriage and the illusion of happiness — Ceremonies, vows, and the
meaning of marriage — Failed marriages — Dissolving the marriage.
    ISBN 1–59102–152–9
    1. Marriage. I. Title.

HQ519.T39 2003
306.81—dc22

                                                                                2003026191

Printed in the United States of America on acid-free paper

contents

Preface   7

Introduction   9

1. MARRIAGE AND THE
ILLUSION OF HAPPINESS   11

The Changing Norms of Marriage   11
Conventional Marriage   19
The Elusive Happiness   22
Marriage as Humdrum   29
Control   34
Why Marriage?   39

2. CEREMONIES, VOWS, AND THE
MEANING OF MARRIAGE   47

Courtship   47
The Wedding   52

The Second Time Around 54
Prenuptial Agreements 56
The Meaning of Marriage 59
Love and the Sense of Self-Worth 64
Married Love 67
Divorce and Friendship 76
Being in Love 82
Sex and Marriage 84

3. FAILED MARRIAGES 87

Why Marriages Fail 87
Sudden Success 91
Infidelity 93
The Penalty for Guilt 99

4. DISSOLVING THE MARRIAGE 103

The Divorce Revolution 103
First Level: Warfare 106
Second Level: Arbitration 113
Third Level: Standard Mediation 119
Fourth Level: Open Mediation 128
    Winning 133
    Guidelines 137
    Magnanimity 145
Fifth Level: Self-Managed Divorce 150

Additional Resources 165

preface

No happiness compares with that which can arise from marriage. Fame, celebrity, and wealth cannot compare with this and are, besides, unstable foundations for any kind of happiness; they can be swept away, sometimes at a stroke. The kind of fulfillment that can arise from a truly good marriage, on the other hand, is limited only by human mortality.

This is the conclusion I have arrived at after many years of studying marriage and talking, often in depth, with married people, especially those long-married.

But notice that I have said, "can arise." Such happiness by no means follows automatically from getting married. On the contrary, it is rare. Half of all marriages collapse in failure, and many of those that do not, struggle against failure. The reasons for this are not hard to discern, and in the pages that follow I try to expose them.

That elusive marital happiness must, of course, rest upon something, and that "something" is not vows, ceremonies, compromise, or any of the other devices people have developed for getting along. It rests upon abiding love. But this concept has been so trivialized and romanticized that a correct understanding of it is virtually non-existent. I have undertaken to explain just what it is.

It is common today to find the alarming rate of divorce countered by trying to make divorce more difficult and inducing faltering couples to "work" on what remains of their marriages. The time to work on a marriage is not when it begins to falter, however. It must begin from the very first day and then continue on, indefinitely. Working on your marriage will consist, in this sense, of cultivating a constant awareness of your partner, of his or her needs and feelings from one moment to the next, and appreciating what will be extensively described as a universal sense of self-worth. No marriage can deliver genuine happiness without this, on both sides.

Thus you do not become married just by having a wedding and filing documentation with the town clerk. That is only the first step. Then you will, if you are lucky and willing to do what is necessary, gradually become married, possibly over the course of years, and reap the kind of happiness that transcends every other. That work of becoming married is not onerous; on the contrary, no task could be more pleasant and rewarding, for you will thus come to know, in the fullest sense, and to appreciate, your lifelong partner.

introduction

arriage is good, divorce is bad. Therefore, people assume, it should be a matter of public policy to encourage marriage and make divorce difficult. In fact, marriage is not always good, and divorce is not always bad. Sometimes marriage is a living hell, and probably most marriages just limp along.

To be sure marriage is sometimes good, and rarely, a source of deep fulfillment, but it is not always good, and most marriages seem to fall quite short of the great good that we like to imagine. And to be sure, divorce is usually bad, a source of deep anger and resentment, surpassing in bitterness every other form of litigation according to attorneys. But not all divorce is bad, and sometimes, though rarely, it can be a true blessing, even, oddly enough, enhancing affection, as we shall see.

The conventional wisdom that divides marriage and divorce into the boxes of good and evil often gives rise to decidedly counterproductive policies. Formal marriage is always easy, requiring little more that the wishes of the partners judicially authenticated, and divorce is always hard, sometimes approaching the impossible, requiring expensive litigation. You need no permission to marry, beyond purchasing a license, but you do need governmental permission to dissolve a marriage. You must satisfy certain requirements, sometimes severe ones, established by law.

It is common for institutions that influence policy to give blanket encouragements to marriage, from the pulpit, for example. Lovers determined to marry, sometimes ready to rush headlong into marriage, are encouraged and praised. There are even governmental programs devised to encourage marriage, such as provisions for joint ownership of property, advantageous health insurance premiums, tax breaks, and so on. Indeed, it has even been proposed to pay people to marry, thereby increasing the numbers and lessening the incidence of single parenthood.

It is extremely doubtful whether such policies do any good at all. People can be encouraged to marry, but there is nothing in these efforts to foster stable, rewarding marriage. True marriage does not rest upon the saying of vows and the filing of documents.

It should also be obvious that making divorce more difficult does nothing to foster happiness. To virtually force an unhappy couple to put up with each other only exacerbates the misery they already feel.

The stereotypical conception of divorce, as always undesirable, can even have absurd complications. For example, heeding this notion, a state legislator proposed that in the case of any divorce the partner who leaves the marriage should forfeit any economic reward, such as alimony, the money thus forfeited going into the state treasury. This was wisely defeated when it was pointed out that, under such a provision, a woman who would flee an abusive and violent husband would be penalized.

What is needed, to foster human happiness and marital stability, is first of all a truer conception of what marriage really is. This book, including accounts taken from interviews and other information I've picked up over the years, is an attempt at this.

chapter 1

marriage and the illusion of happiness

THE CHANGING NORMS OF MARRIAGE

Both marriage and divorce have undergone radical change. Divorce was, until quite recently, entirely the province of lawyers and was thus cast as an adversarial proceeding. Now it is increasingly dealt with through mediation, the role of lawyers being reduced to little more than a clerical function. With this shift has come a huge change in the way divorce is thought of. We almost never think of it as involving a wronged and innocent party versus a guilty one, and almost never do divorced people suffer opprobrium or loss of status. Laws now reflect this change, too, for in almost every jurisdiction divorce can be granted for what simply amounts to marital failure. No one really needs any longer to prove that one or the other partner is to blame for anything.

It is not the same with marriage. It, too, is undergoing great change, cohabitation becoming more and more common and acceptable. And yet, our conception of what it means to be married has hardly changed at all. We still think that people become married at a stroke, as a result of a customary ceremony, often elaborately staged, and that they then remain married until formally divorced. And we still think of the love, which is assumed to underlie all good marriages, as a kind of deep passion, sometimes of sudden occurrence, that leads to courtship, and then marriage.

Both of these conceptions are seriously wrong. Marriage, if it is to have any significant meaning, is *not* a status that is conferred by the enunciation of vows and a pronouncement by a presiding official, and "getting married" does *not*, except in the most superficial sense, mean having a wedding. Similarly, love is *not* something that one falls into, and the passions associated with that word are not the basis of any meaningful marriage.

Here, to illustrate this, is the customary conception of marriage.

First, it is thought, a man and a woman fall in love, often with great suddenness, even "at first sight." This love grows, becomes a bond between them, and is seen by them and everyone else as providing the basis for a marriage that will last until they are separated by death. Engagement follows, symbolized by a ring, often an expensive one, bestowed by the man, thought of as a suitor. Next, at an agreed-upon date, and often with long, laborious, and costly preparations, they are joined in marriage, typically to the accompaniment of an elaborate and expensive ceremony, the bride's "hand" being given over to the groom by her father, who, by custom, bears the cost of all this. The transition, from the status of being single to that of being married persons, now occurs with great suddenness, when the presiding cleric, after eliciting solemn vows of fidelity from each, intones the words "I now pronounce you man and wife." Now they have a totally new status. They are a married couple. Joyous music bursts forth, bride and groom retreat slowly down the aisle, beaming with joy, past a sometimes large gathering of witnesses to this sudden and profound transition, the attendees also beaming with joy, or sometimes, weeping with mixed joy and sadness. A reception follows, sometimes with dancing, enhanced by a table laden with wedding gifts. According to tradition, the two then disappear, on a honeymoon, joyously celebrating their new and momentous status and, according to tradition at least, now consummate their marriage with paroxysms of joy and sexual intimacy, once assumed to be a novel experience for both.

What is significant in all this, quite apart from all the accompanying extravagance, is that virtually everyone in our culture believes that this is what it means to become a married person. You get married by having a wedding of some sort. And the transition, from unmarried to married, occurs in an instant. Stories have sometimes been woven around the image of one of these two, most likely the bride, suddenly fleeing just before the magic words are spoken and thus narrowly escaping that status, with all its limitations and expectations.

All this is a myth, an elaborate fabric of errors, nourished by romantic notions that have little to do with life.

People can become married without any of those things happening, and, what is perhaps more surprising, every detail of that picture can be fulfilled *without any marriage having occurred.*

For example, in some jurisdictions a couple can become married simply by cohabiting for a considerable time, the so-called common-law marriage. There need be no wedding, no vows, no ceremony of any kind. Such marriages are not recognized as such in some jurisdictions, but they are in others, where both husband and wife enjoy all the legal protections of marriage having to do with property, custody of children, inheritance, and so on. Indeed, as we shall see later, this is without a doubt a far more rational conception of what it means to be married than the mythological one just sketched.

But going further, it can be seen that the sometimes elaborate procedures just described are not even *sufficient* for establishing a marriage. A couple can do all of the ceremonial things, including a formal wedding duly presided over by a clergyperson, and so on, and still not be married, even in the minimal sense of legality.

For a marriage to have the status of legitimacy, permission to marry must be granted by the state. This takes the form of a license to marry, and certain conditions are placed on the issuance of such a document. Typically, each applicant must submit to medical tests to prove freedom from certain diseases. A waiting period is then imposed, usually at least twenty-four hours, in order to insure sobriety as the couple approaches the altar. Further, a person presiding over such a ceremony must be legally entitled to do so, a power vested in that person by the state. He or she must have been ordained as a minister or rabbi, for example, or else have met the requirements of judicial office, such as that of justice of the peace. And finally, the marriage must be certified and recorded in some hall of records. This usually means that the person who presided over the ceremony certifies on the marriage license that it did occur, at such and such time and place, and this person then files it with the recognized hall of records, typically the town clerk.

It is not difficult to see that failure can occur at any of these points. Suppose, for example, that the presiding person is a self-styled minister, never ordained, and without any such power vested in him by government. No matter how grand the wedding and the accompanying ceremonies, that marriage will have no legal validity whatever, even if never challenged. Or suppose the wedding is performed by a justice of the peace whose commission has expired, and who, therefore, has no more authority to pronounce anyone married than any other person who comes down the street. Or suppose that a wedding is presided over by an ordained clergyman, who meets all of the legal requirements for authority to perform such a ceremony, but that certification of this somehow fails to arrive at the hall of records. A critical step toward legalization of the union will then have failed to have happened, even though, once again, the validity of the marriage may never be questioned. (If it were, then the challenge could probably be met by producing an album of wedding pictures or something of this sort.) And finally, what if the couple thus joined happen to be of the same sex. Such a union will not be recognized as a marriage, and indeed no license to marry will even be issued, although in a very few jurisdictions the relationship thus created will be deemed a "civil union," having all or most of the legal rights of a married couple, such as the right to obtain family coverage of health insurance, adopt children, inherit property, and so on.

If the foregoing seems to be hair-splitting legalisms, then consider the following case:

> We decided to have a minister we both knew and liked do our wedding, but when we approached him on this he said that he took very seriously the separation of church and state and that, in light of this, while he would be glad to preside over our wedding, with all the usual vows and ceremony, we would then have to find a justice of the peace to legalize it. What we wanted was a proper wedding, in a church, like everyone else, and not some tacky procedure by a justice of the peace we didn't even know, and we wanted this minister to do it, so we went along with this idea, partly because we, too, believe strongly in the separation of church and state. The wedding went off exactly as we had planned and hoped, with the customary vows, reception, and everything, the only difference being, as the minister pointed out, that he omitted the words, "by the authority vested in me by the state" before saying "I now pronounce you man and wife." No one noticed this, however, and everyone just took for granted that we were now husband and wife. That all happened ten years ago. We at first intended to find a justice of the peace, to make it legal, but never got around to it, so in truth, we are still not married. In fact, we never even bothered to get a marriage license. This hasn't made any difference in our relationship; we certainly *feel* married, and very happily so, and everyone thinks we are. Our children have their father's last name, as I do, and by this time we see no point in legalizing things. We own all our property together, have joint wills, hold each other's health proxies, and we each have power of attorney for the other. We have no need to file joint tax returns, we each have our own health insurance,

and so cannot be accused of using our make-believe marriage dishonestly. And all this has made us wonder, what is marriage, anyway: would we be *more* married if we now looked up some justice of the peace?

This sort of example does indeed raise the philosophical question of what it really means to be married. The fact that a man and a woman can have a lasting relationship with every semblance of marriage but one which is, from the standpoint of the law, no more than cohabitation, does lead one to question the importance of legality in this area. What is even more to the point, however, is that a man and a woman can fulfill every requirement of having gotten married—all the legal details met, wedding celebrated, with all of the attendant ceremonies, and still *not* be married in any significant sense. This is something that people find hard to accept. We think in stereotypes, in absolute distinctions of either married, or not married, and if a man and a woman are not legally married, we think, then they are mere friends, or just people cohabiting.

The mere legality of a marriage is not sufficient for the creation of a genuine marital state, for there is vastly more to being married than merely having fulfilled the requirements of law. Notwithstanding popular belief, marriage is not something that happens with suddenness. People *become* married, over time. Sometimes—very often, in fact—what promised to be a marriage becomes instead a dead marriage, even without the legality of divorce, and a dead marriage is no more still a marriage than a dead cat is still a cat.

The defense of this will be taken up later, but for now, consider how, in very realistic terms, a union of man and a woman can fail to be a genuine marriage, quite apart from any rituals and legalities that created that relationship:

We were graduate students and had become close friends. I was an American citizen by birth, while she was a citizen of Brazil. She had for some time planned to become an American citizen and pursue a lifetime career here, when she got the idea that, if I were to marry her, citizenship would follow automatically. I at that point had no expectation of marrying anyone, whether then or thereafter, nor did she, but it seemed to both of us that this might be the simplest and best route to citizenship. We talked about it with great care, both agreeing that we would remain, at most, friends, and that neither of us would have any expectations beyond that. So that's what we did. We got the marriage license and found a justice of the peace to marry us, without ceremony or publicity. Only a few of our friends knew about this, and they didn't make anything of it. That all happened six years ago. We both finished our studies and moved far away from each other. I've seen her a couple of times since, for we are still friends of a sort, but we almost never write or communicate in any other way. If either of us should ever decide to get really married, not to each other, of course, then I suppose we'll need to dissolve this marriage, if it can be called that, but so far that problem has not come up.

That sort of thing is far more common than people realize, for it is a very tempting route to citizenship. It is seldom that easy, however, for when there is suspicion of such collusion, then there is apt to be an investigation by the Immigration and Naturalization Service (INS) in which the parties are subjected to serious questioning intended to elicit whether they were merely using the law to gain citizenship that might otherwise be difficult to obtain. Still, it can succeed, and when it does we can ask the very serious question: Is the legality of a marriage sufficient to create a genuine marriage? And the answer seems plainly to be no.

Other examples come readily to mind. Thus, what if a man or a woman marries only to gain control of the wealth of the other person? This does sometimes happen. In one case that attracted considerable attention a man married a wealthy widow with advanced Alzheimer's disease. He was roundly castigated in the press as a scoundrel and gold digger, but he protested that love was his only motive, and that it had nothing to do with money. And the law was perfectly clear: she was his wife, and he the heir to her fortune. But again we ask: Were they really married? It surely is at least doubtful.

Or again, what of a couple whose marriage is never consummated, and who, finding they have nothing whatever in common, drift apart, to the point that they almost never see or correspond with each other, although they still file joint tax returns and so on. Are they really married? Surely one can say, hardly.

In the Roman Catholic Church marriage is never dissolved through divorce, as this would violate canon law, but annulments are often granted, sometimes on what seem to be trivial or contrived grounds. Thus, while a couple may have met all the legal requirements of marriage, and appeared to meet those of the church as well, and may even have adult children by that marriage, it can be annulled because, for example, one or the other partner did not have a correct understanding of what marriage is when the wedding was performed, or was perhaps not baptized at the time, or had had a vasectomy, or whatever. This is not to imply that annulment of marriage is easy; it can be difficult and time-consuming. But what this does mean is that, from the standpoint of the church, that marriage never existed, even though its legality is beyond question, and even though its partners may have lived as a married couple for many years and even had children together.

Thus, from the standpoint of the church, it takes more to create a marriage than compliance with civil law, and what may even appear to be a marriage in every sense can turn out to have been no marriage at all.

What can we conclude from all this? Very simply, that marriage cannot be understood just in terms of custom and law. We must turn instead to philosophy. It will be the purpose in the pages that follow to gain a more workable and intelligent conception of marriage, and thus lay the groundwork for understanding what it takes to create a good and lasting marriage, and to gain the kind of happiness that marriage sometimes, albeit rarely, makes possible.

CONVENTIONAL MARRIAGE

While the basic and stereotypical concept of being married has not changed much, marriage itself has undergone vast changes since about the middle of the twentieth century. Prior to that change marriage was characterized by a clear distinction of roles. The husband supplied the financial foundation while the wife was the homemaker. For a wife to be gainfully employed amounted to her husband shirking his responsibilities. A real concern of a bride's parents was whether the man she wanted to marry could properly support her. Married women sometimes had secondary incomes, but they were not supposed to be thought of as needing them. She perhaps raised chickens, and the egg money was hers, or she accepted secretarial work, or community work for which she was nominally paid, but there was nothing wrong with her quitting if she felt like it or choosing to avoid gainful work altogether. Not so for her husband. He did not have that choice at all, and if his wife worked he was disparagingly thought of as having "put her out to work," clearly implying that she did not really belong there at all. The professions, with the exception of teaching, most typically teaching small children, were virtually closed to women. There were very few female physicians, and virtually all nurses were women. There were few female college professors, and at least some women's colleges boasted in their public relations of the numbers of men on their faculties. There were virtually no female attorneys, or even veterinarians or clergy. A woman's status in the community was mostly a reflection of her husband's position, very high if, for example, he was a physician, less so, for example, if he was the proprietor of the local pool hall, even if he prospered. While men joined professional associations, their wives were mostly restricted to "ladies' auxiliaries."

Child-rearing was mostly reserved for the mother, and in the case of divorce, custody was almost automatically awarded to her. The divorced husband's responsibility was alimony—a word that is now seldom used. The mother was the source of tenderness, and the father more likely the ultimate disciplinarian, looked to by the rest with a certain awe. Middle-class men and women were expected to maintain this image in their public behavior and dress. Men of standing did not appear in public without a necktie, and women were never to dress in a manner suggestive of immodesty.

All of this did not necessarily imply a subjugation of women. It was just custom. A wife was responsible for the home, for example. All this was considered *hers*, and a source of pride. It was she who mostly determined matters having to do with décor, and also she who planned meals, kept the household budget, and so on. To the extent that her husband participated in these things—cooking or doing the dishes, for example—then this was thought of as "helping."

Contemporary men look upon this model of marriage with amusement, perhaps nostalgic longing, while women view it with horror. To them it looks like the institutionalization of a woman's inferior status. And indeed few today, with the exception of the very conservative who style themselves "pro-family," would consider returning to it. And yet marriage was, in that bygone age, quite stable. People did for the most part remain together until parted by death. To a large extent, of course, this was due to social pressure. A divorced man was to some extent considered shamed, the more so if he then remarried; and a divorced woman tended to be thought of as secondhand goods, the now archaic term for her being "relict."

Yet there is another side to this, and that is that these traditional marriages were often deeply fulfilling to both husband and wife, and they remained in them because of a genuine bond of love between them. Needs were often met. The husband's sense of worth was found in his work, and, if successful there, he was looked up to by both his family and the community. He was respected, even though his worldly achievements may have been modest. More important, very often the wife's needs were met, too. She did not look upon *work* as a great good that was denied her. That was a man's world. Her fulfillments were more likely to be in her home, where she was sovereign. Her husband did not feel excluded from this. That was the woman's world. She raised the children, her husband more or less standing as the final disciplinarian, and both took deep pride in them when they turned out well. Father was looked up to with a certain awe, but mother was venerated. It was common for very successful men to attribute their achievements to their mothers, who were officially celebrated by a special Mother's Day. Father's Day came later, and was largely due to commercialization rather than social attitudes.

The foregoing is not meant as a glorification of the traditional marriage. There was lots wrong with it, notwithstanding the nostalgia of conservatives. It was hardly surprising to find that not all marriages fit that picture. And yet marriages like that did exist, and were happy, and now we raise the important question: *Why?* Just what is that bond of love that nourished such happiness?

It was not, certainly, the romantic love that led them into the marriage. Romantic love is a passion. It is the love that is celebrated in song and poetry, that is intense, and often represented as instantaneous—that "walks right in and brings one's happiest day" and so on. Sometimes it is described as a *chemistry* between two people, a kind of reaction that arises powerfully and suddenly, but is ignited with no one else but the "one and only." It is all very familiar and, to be sure, adds much zest and excitement to life, especially when felt for the first time.

It is sad indeed, however, that this is also naively thought of as the love that will unite a couple forever. A couple betrothed and in love imagine that because the emotion is so intense, then it will also be lasting.

It does not take long, however, for this romantic love to be replaced by something quite different, sometimes by what we shall call *married love*, but very often by disappointments and even disillusion. The husband who is frugal discovers that his wife is given to extravagance, producing almost daily annoyances. Or the wife finds that her husband, who was so considerate and ingratiating before, turns out to be controlling. She might find that his slovenly habits, of which she was only dimly aware before, are a fixed part of his personality: he leaves dirty clothes scattered around, goes unshaven, puts off doing the simplest chores. Perhaps he turns out to be a womanizer. Having captured her, he is now more charmed by every other woman he meets. He might find that she is given to frivolous pursuits, talking endlessly on the telephone to no purpose, or reading trashy novels, and so on.

The possibilities are endless, and they all throw a profound damper on the romantic love that now evaporates. Perhaps, dimly aware of his shortcomings, she thought she could change him, and he was under the same wishful thinking. They do not change. Once married, their shortcomings just become more apparent. She was able to conceal the things he didn't like until then, and he, having now induced her to marry him, can similarly relax. There is no longer any *need to* set aside faults. Now each can be himself or herself. And very likely, the marriage is headed for failure. Indeed, it has already failed in the only sense that matters; that is, the love that was supposed to unite them dies, and with it, the marriage, even when there are forces at work that preclude divorce.

Of course things do not always turn out that way. There *are* happy marriages. There are even marriages whose partners have the greatest happiness that human beings can find, although these are rare.

And now we must ask: What is it that yields this success? What is the source of such happiness? It is, of course, abiding love. But if this is not the romantic love that evaporates, and should evaporate, then what is it? I have already alluded to it as *married love*, but have so far given no hint as to what this is.

THE ELUSIVE HAPPINESS

It is generally believed, at least among the unmarried, that marriage is a path to great happiness. Indeed it can be, but sadly, it seldom is.

The fact that a marriage has a fifty-fifty chance of ending in divorce is proof that conventional marriage has failed. To be sure, partners do often get along, not even thinking of divorce, but too often their happiness, such as it is, arises from sources outside the marriage itself—from careers, common pursuits, children, and so on. The rejoicing that accompanied the start of a marriage—the ceremony, the music, the feasting and gifts—is supposed to portend a deep happiness that all too often never comes. Surely the institution of marriage, so basic to social stability, needs to be rethought. We need a clearer, more philosophical conception of what it *means* to be married, to replace the legalistic and conventional one that now prevails. Merely going before a preacher and enunciating vows does not make a marriage.

It is the primary theme of this book that the happiness that *can* arise from marriage is unique, deep, and indestructible. No other happiness compares with it, and those relatively few who have it would not trade it for the most enviable status on earth. Wealth, power, celebrity—things like this offer little in comparison with the enduring happiness of loving and being loved to the very end of life.

What, then, must marriage be in order for this to be true? Before addressing that large question, we need a closer look at the dismal status of contemporary marriages.

If half of such marriages are so bad that they end in divorce, what about the other half? Shall we call them happy marriages? Hardly. These are marriages that have survived, but that is by itself no measure of happiness.

We can illustrate this graphically as follows:

The bar above represents a sampling of marriages. The line in the middle separates those that end in divorce from those that do not. The intensity of black represents the degree of unhappiness, the marriages symbolized at the right being so miserable that they are terminated, often at great cost.

Since the marriages here symbolized represent a true sampling (a random sampling), the bar shows a continuum with respect to the degrees of happiness or unhappiness found in those marriages. The left half cannot be all white. Genuine marital happiness, of the kind I discuss, is in fact rare—even among those who say they are "happy." People do not want to admit that the marriages they are stuck in are dead. I find this over and over. The bar gives the true picture of things.

To make matters even worse, the dividing line in the middle cannot be a sharp one, because deeply unhappy marriages neverthe-less often survive, being held together, not by the fulfillment of its partners, but by extraneous forces, such as religion, children, and often by sheer inertia. Thus, partners who somehow remain married are sometimes more miserable than those who do not.

Couples who are not happy in their marriages still have many rea-sons for sticking things out, one of them always being simply the dif-ficulties, legal and other, of divorce. It is very easy to get married, but usually hard to get out, for a great variety of reasons—children, prop-erty, religion, social pressure and especially, sheer inertia.

Of course none of this should be understood to mean that mar-riage is a worthless institution or utterly without social value. Mar-riage is important for social stability, for the sharing and transfer of property, and above all, for the health and security of children. And it is clearly for reasons such as these that there are laws to protect it. No laws can make marriages happy, however. One reason we are led to think that marriage will yield deep and lasting happiness is to pre-serve the institution for reasons having little to do with happiness. So the myth is nourished that the romantic love that leads people to the altar portends lasting happiness, when it in fact is perhaps the most ephemeral of all strong passions. A couple, once joined in wed-lock, having vowed to love each other forever, are serenaded, again from the same motive. Marriage, though it rarely delivers the happiness promised, must, it is thought, nevertheless be promoted, just because social life would be much worse off without it. It is a heavy burden to lay upon the guileless and innocent victims.

From our graphic representation we can see that if divorce were made impossible, as some would have it, then there would be no dividing line in our bar. This clearly would not, however, reduce the amount of black there. On the contrary, it would increase it, for the partners thus forced to remain married would, for that very reason, suffer even more, being in effect prisoners within a detested union, and thereby denied the possibility of making things better, perhaps with new partners.

Divorce is bad, no doubt, but the solution is not to make it harder. It is highly destructive for the Roman Catholic Church, for example, to pressure lawmakers to outlaw it even for those who do not share that faith. It would not preserve marriage, except for appearance, but would have the opposite effect upon marriage if this is thought of as an ethical ideal.

If there is so much unhappiness in marriage, then why is it not apparent? Most married people seem to be happy and in fact declare that they are. How can this be squared with what has just been said, and with the picture conveyed by our graph?

The answer is that we are here speaking of different sources of happiness. Yes, many married people are reasonably happy, but their happiness arises from sources other than the marriage itself. And these are numerous.

For example, an older man of great wealth and status marries someone whose chief attributes are youth and beauty. He is not seeking happiness that arises from the kind of married love that is unique and indestructible. Rather, he wants someone who will further enhance his status and, perhaps, help him recover a sense of youth. Such wives are appropriately called "trophy wives." Her incentive, on the other hand, is likely to be the allure of wealth and status, instantly and effortlessly bestowed. And both partners might in fact get what they are seeking, at least up to a point, and find satisfaction in this, so that they can honestly declare that they are "happy." But clearly, they do not have the kind of happiness that we have been speaking of here, the indestructible happiness of loving and being loved forever. In fact, such unions are notoriously unstable and often end disastrously and with much publicity.

Again, married people sometimes find greater happiness in raising their children than in each other. This is very good for the children, and to a point, good for the marriage, too. But children grow up and, when they have left, husband and wife are apt to find that they have little in common to keep them together.

Some couples make what amount to financial partnerships of their marriage, cooperating in the pursuit of a common goal that each would find hard to reach without the other. Typical of this kind of marriage is one where they have the same professional careers— both are physicians, practicing together, for example, or they are both attorneys whose specialties differ but reinforce each other. Such couples have a very strong foundation for their marriage, in a kind of symbiotic relationship, and can honestly cite this as a source of happiness. Still, it is not a happiness that arises just from the marriage.

Another possibility, a couple whose love for each other is long since dead are very likely not to rush into divorce simply because the arrangement they have built up over the years appears to them to be better than going their separate ways. They have shared the same roof for so long that it would not be worth changing things, even though they may have ceased sharing the same bed, or even if they have ceased to have a deep interest in each other. Still, they might declare, sincerely, that they have a happy marriage, meaning by this little beyond the fact that it has endured and they have adjusted to it all.

One thing that is not significant in holding otherwise weak marriages together is sex. It may be, as some have thought, that sexual attraction is what drives people into marriage, but certainly it does not by itself keep them there. This is so for two reasons. First of all, sexual passion, though it may remain as a strong and vital expression of love, nevertheless diminishes as a blind urge, and second, sexual intimacy can never hold together an otherwise moribund marriage. When other things holding a marriage together go, so does this one. When love is gone, then the passion that may have brought lovers together in the first place dies, too. What creates abiding love is not sex, but the multitude of lesser needs that are met, and when these are not met, everything else goes as well. This is a rather large claim, but the defense of it must wait.

What we have described as the factors that hold weak marriages together are, it is important to note, mostly small things, to which we must add that they are also compatible with the kind of enduring love that forms the basis for marriage in its deeper sense. The best of marriages would be poorer without them. Still, they are fragile bonds, and have little to do with marriage itself, for they can as easily occur outside of marriage, in ordinary friendships.

Religion is sometimes cited as a bulwark of marriage. "Families that pray together stay together"—we have all heard this. It is a common pitch for religion, an attempt to bring the "unchurched" into the fold.

Do we have here, then, a means of reducing the divorce rate? If more people could be led into church, would that strengthen their marriages? It is very doubtful. For in the first place, this is an example of the classic fallacy of *post hoc, ergo propter hoc*—the fallacy, that is, of supposing that if two things are regularly correlated, then one must be the cause of the other. Thus, it is assumed that if religious people stay married and the nonreligious do not, then it must be that religion is what holds them together.

What is far more likely is that the kind of person who takes religion very seriously is also the kind of person who takes marriage very seriously. Such a person is apt to be conservative in his or her social values, and conventional with respect to established social norms. And it is that kind of person who is likely to take marriage, and what are thought of as traditional "family values," seriously.

There is no reason whatsoever to suppose, then, that persons of a different temperament will stabilize their marriage *just* by being induced to attend church.

The fallacy can be illustrated in other examples. For instance, we know that persons living in the southern United States are more likely to speak with a drawl than northerners. It does not follow, however, that if we could induce northerners to move south, then they would speak with a drawl. Or again, vegetarians are likely also to be environmentalists, but we cannot conclude that if, for health reasons, for example, we could induce more people to adopt a vegetarian diet, then this would give a boost to environmental concerns. Things can go hand in hand without being causally related, for correlations are often the result of some third variable.

But quite apart from that, there is no reason to think that religious people are more happily married than others. The same factors that make for happy marriages are found among both the religious and the nonreligious, and conversely, the same factors that contribute to marital strife are found among both. So even if the divorce rate could be reduced by the promotion of religion, which is plainly doubtful to begin with, this would not by itself result in happier marriages. Even marriages that last can be filled with frustration and unhappiness, and sometimes, even misery.

The following anecdote, comical on the surface, conceals a deep bitterness:

> I was at the photographer's to order pictures for our fortieth wedding anniversary when a woman came in to make the same arrangement for her fiftieth anniversary. Hearing this, the clerk gushed, "Oh Honey! That must have been wonderful," to which the woman responded, "Oh Honey! It was nothing but hell!"

Surely the goal of anyone seeking to strengthen marriage should be, first of all, to make marriages happier, and more lasting for that reason, and not merely to make them somehow more lasting.

MARRIAGE AS HUMDRUM

The clearest mark of a failed marriage is, of course, a divorce, but as we have already noted, marriages can fail without ending in divorce. It is all too common. There is no way of knowing just how common, but our earlier bar illustration provides a suggestion. Marriages die. Some of the dead marriages end in divorce, but, for numerous reasons already discussed, many do not.

There are many couples who live together, as they have for years, with no thought of divorce and often with no hint of failed marriage, even though their marriages have in fact ended in failure in the one sense that really matters—their love for each other has died. It has not turned to hatred, so common among the divorced, but it still is no longer there. These couples are likely to do, year after year, what they have always done—dine out together, visit their children or grandchildren, have cookouts with friends, and maintain all the established relationships. And yet, they have little interest in each other beyond those accustomed pursuits. They do not talk with each other much on social occasions, but instead drift to others. Each is likely to have a circle of friends in which the other has no interest and hence no part. They are husband and wife, thought of by all as such, and respected as such. Yet, in truth, they have no deep love for each other, have little interest in what each other is doing, and go on with their lives in the accustomed manner. They don't discuss their feelings, their fears and anxieties, or their innermost thoughts, and, indeed, they are not much given to these anyway. So they do not talk to each other much, either, except about passing things. And, most important, neither ever thinks of divorce. They have grown accustomed to things the way they are.

Of the dozens of people with failed or faltering marriages that I have interviewed, the most common description that women gave of their husbands was that they were "boring." What this invariably meant was that their husbands were too wrapped up in themselves to pay much attention to them. And the next most common complaint was that their husbands were "controlling." And yet, what was surprising was that these marriages often went right on as before, notwithstanding the fact they were all marriages that were in trouble. In some cases the partners had even separated, and then ruefully gone back to each other. The marriages were for the most part dead, but the alternatives were even worse. Even dead marriages usually have much to keep them afloat, especially marriages of long standing, and the main factor in this is probably sheer inertia. A radical change in one's life is not easy to deal with, especially as we grow older.

Here, for example, are some samples of humdrum marriages, not all of which ended in divorce:

> Our home life resembles two ships passing in the night. We're living there in the same house, which is beautifully located, but rather isolated, so much of the time we have only each other for company, but we are not company. Whole days go by with my husband hardly noticing me; he's just doing his own things, more or less as if I were not even there. I like to play the piano, but if I do, he asks me to stop, because it disturbs his concentration. Mostly if he speaks to me at all it is to find fault with something. Our children are grown and far away, so we no longer are raising them together. Our comings and goings are determined by him, and his schedule. I can never simply announce that I'm going someplace. He has to make the final decision.

That is a marriage in which there is no easily recognizable fault. There was no overt abuse, no infidelity, nothing like that. It was a dead marriage. When I asked her why she stayed in it, she just pointed out the indisputable fact that she had no real choice— nowhere to go and no security outside the marriage. She was simply stuck. And yet, the two were everywhere accepted as a long married and highly respected couple. The flaws described here were not generally known, but were confided to me.

We were married for twenty-five years, and during that whole time it seemed to me that my ideas never counted, that I simply was not heard. My husband would propose—or rather announce—something, and I was expected to just go along. If I suggested something else, he usually didn't even respond. For example, we needed a new front door, and I suggested that it be a glass one. He said nothing, but when we got the door it did turn out to be a glass one. It didn't usually work out that way. When he announced that he was going to mow near the garden, I asked him to be careful not to mow the raspberry plants I had just planted. He just mowed them anyway, as if I had said nothing. The same happened with my perennials. Those that were not in straight rows just got plowed under. And it was somehow always up to me to empty the cat box and stoke the fire in the morning. He never offered. It seemed to me that I was always sort of at the edge of everything. Once, when we were driving off to the dump, I indicated that I preferred not to go, but instead of dropping me off, he just drove on, as if I had said nothing, and I had to jump from the moving car. We had some old huts out in back, which had been there when we bought the property, and I wanted them removed. They were ugly and unused. Nothing was ever done about this; they're probably still there.

It is worth noting that this husband, after his wife had left, sometimes tearfully begged her to come back, though there was no indication that anything would change if she did. His needs had been met, even though hers had not.

What is significant here is the extreme banality, even triviality, of the needs not met. It was not that they were poor, or hungry, or in bad health, or that either was unfaithful, and no blows were ever struck. These basic needs were all fulfilled. It was just the small, seemingly petty ones that were not. It made the wife feel unimportant to her husband, and indeed, unloved, and that perception was entirely correct. For love simply *is* the fulfillment of needs—not just the basic ones, but also the little, day-to-day ones.

It is a lesson that too few ever learn. Our self-centeredness tends to blind us to the needs of partners. And the result is that marriages fail. Even those that do not end in divorce often fail, for the success of a marriage is measured by its happiness, not by its duration.

> We have a nice, neatly kept house, and no one would suspect that ours is anything but a stable and even happy marriage. We have a more-than-adequate income, a good social life, and my parents think that my husband is just perfect for me. Before we were married he was totally attentive, driving almost every day a round trip of almost two hundred miles just to be with me. But that didn't last after we were married. He simply takes me for granted and seems hardly aware of me most of the time. He never has any idea what I am thinking or feeling and no interest in finding out. If he's having a beer and I say I'd like a glass of wine, he sets the bottle out and walks off; it would not occur to him to pour it for me. If we have guests for a hamburger cookout, he is totally solicitous of how everyone wants theirs prepared—except for me. Once, when he said he was going out for a six-pack, I asked him to bring me a very mild beer. He brought the darkest, most awful brew you can imagine, as if he hadn't even heard me. That's what our life is like. But I'll never leave him. He is totally trustworthy, stable, and my life's security.

That woman kept her emotional life intact by having an ongoing affair with a musician, and she considered this to be a major stabilizing factor in her marriage. What she did not get from her husband she got from him—attention, to every detail of the commonplace things that were important to her.

> We've been married twenty years and for a long time we've both been planning divorce, but we never talk about it. We don't talk about anything, and that's been going on for a long time.
>   I got pregnant soon after we were married, and I was sorry I did, because I could see even then that the marriage was not good. That's our only child, and she's now eighteen. She is, for

me, the only reason we're still married, because I have read how children are damaged by divorce.

My husband's feeling toward me is complete indifference, if that can be called a feeling, and it has been that way from the beginning. I am routinely ignored, to the point that now complete silence is the rule. We all three have dinner together almost every night, but he says nothing. Neither do I. We even still sleep in the same bed, but it is totally without affection or even acknowledging each other's presence.

His disregard for me eventually turned to constant anger. I long ago learned that it was pointless to ask him for anything. If I asked him to pick something up for me at the store, he would claim he was not going that way, even though in fact he was. He seemed to go out of his way to show his disregard. One day, when a phone call came for him and he was away, I left a note for him, fearing that I might forget to tell him. He failed to see the note, and blew up at me. That has been the pattern for years. He is always mad, and always controlling. He never tells me where he is, or where he is going. He just gets up and leaves. We have no friends, no social life, but we do usually go out for dinner together on his birthday and again on mine.

This account is a pretty good working definition of hell, and one wonders why, to what purpose, this husband and wife would still dine out on birthdays, or how there could possibly be any joy in such an evening. What is most astonishing of all, however, is that toward the end of the interview this beautiful but damaged person said she was quite aware that for years her husband had been having an affair, or maybe several. She was so little concerned about this thunderous revelation that she was not even curious to know who it was, and had not even brought it up until the end of our talk.

It is easy to see that all these accounts, together with countless others I could supply, have one thing in common. One of the partners—namely the husband—is too self-absorbed to pay attention to, or even to be very aware of, his wife. There are, of course, strong-willed and controlling wives, too, but there is no doubt that this shortcoming belongs mostly to husbands. And in every case, we can assume, these partners were once *in love* with each other, in the superficial sense of love that people identify with romantic passion. They were sufficiently in love to plan a wedding, with high expectation, then go before a clergyperson and vow to keep that love forever, forsaking all others, and so on. But it didn't mean much once the knot was tied. What was important simply was not there, and probably never had been; namely, an awareness of the day-to-day, even moment-to-moment, ordinary needs of each other. The passionate declarations that led them to the altar did not mean much, because it was not the kind of love that lasts. It was exciting, to be sure, but genuine love is built on small things.

One of the sincerest and purest declarations of love that I have ever heard was this one, from a man who seemed, like his wife, utterly fulfilled: "Me and her, we get along real good." If, in the light of what has been said, you ask what was behind that seemingly passing remark, the answer is not hard to find.

CONTROL

The need to control may be a part of human nature—to control our environment, our working conditions, and, especially, other persons. This also extends into marriage, but it really has no place there. Married people should, ideally, think of themselves as if they were one person, thus avoiding any tendency to the subordination of one to the other.

The urge to control is, without a doubt, more common in men than in women. Men like to be in charge. A man tends to think that the word "my," in "my wife," signifies possession, and thus, the right to control, to make decisions, even in areas in which the wife's needs and interests are clearly equal to his and even, sometimes, obviously more important. Some men simply assume the right to decide where they will vacation, where they will live, how the family income will be spent, what kind of car they shall drive, and so on. There are even cases in which a husband dictates what his wife will wear, or whether she shall use makeup—matters in which, obviously, he should have little or no voice at all.

Of course there are also controlling wives, but they are certainly the exception. A very strong-willed woman married to a weak-willed man is apt to assume the role of decision maker. And fairly often she will assume that role with respect to their children, especially a daughter.

Still, it is far more common for men to want to be in control. This seems not to be a purely cultural matter, either. In some cultures women cannot vote, petition for divorce, or even own property, and this has been true throughout recorded history. The emancipation of women is, in fact, a recent change, and it has been mostly limited to Western industrial countries.

Of course the democratic values upheld in our culture militate against male dominance, as does the force of feminism, but these have not altered marriage very much. When you see a husband and a wife in a car, it is usually the man who is driving. At social gatherings it is usually the husband who announces when it is time to leave. It is usually, also, the man who dominates conversation in such gatherings.

Such division of roles has little significance in small matters such as these. The mere fact that a husband and a wife have different roles does not by itself imply subordination. When a husband assumes the role of doing the cooking, for example, the wife is not likely to feel cast into a secondary position, nor does a husband feel that way if the wife does the cooking. It is in the larger areas, where needs and desires may diverge radically, that control by one partner, usually the male, is destructive.

An effort to correct this imbalance in marriages was made in 1972 by Nena and George O'Neill in their book *Open Marriage*.

Unfortunately this book was almost universally misunderstood. The authors' thesis was simply that marriage should not by itself restrict either partner from developing his or her own interests and potential, and that the wife, especially, should be free from control, that marriage should not make a woman a lesser person in any respect. We tend to regard as normal those marriages, especially lasting ones, in which the wife simply puts her husband first, often at the expense of her own growth as a person. But the book contained one huge blunder. In addressing the question of whether sexual fidelity was compatible with the concept of open marriage, they reluctantly concluded that it need not be, that neither husband nor wife should feel constrained by this long-standing taboo. Readers and reviewers at once assumed that this was the very point of open marriage, that partners should feel utterly free to associate with outsiders of either sex, even to the point of what is generally thought to be the clearest violation of the marital bond. That husbands and wives should feel free to choose their friendships from both sexes is of course obvious, but pursuing such friendship to the point of sexual intimacy is so manifestly destructive of marriage that no logic can make it appear acceptable.

That was the authors' huge mistake, and it is unfortunate, since the basic theme of the book, that marriage should be a relationship that fosters freedom and growth, is clearly correct and important. That important message was simply lost, and the book never had the wholesome impact that it should have.

For a man to control his wife is to violate the most basic requirement of a truly fulfilling marriage, because it is to put his own needs above hers, and, necessarily, to render some of her needs and aspirations impossible of fulfillment. Of course no marriage can be a perfect blending of wills. Some things have to give. But when a husband goes beyond simple lack of awareness of his wife, which is exceedingly common, to the point of overriding even her most urgent needs, then the marriage has passed from being what we have called humdrum to outright abuse, even though no physical blows have been struck. Violence can take many forms, of which physical violence is simply the most extreme.

Here, for example, is an account of the most extreme control, related to me by a highly educated and urbane woman who had allowed herself to become trapped almost to the point of her own destruction. It serves to illustrate the aberrant psychology that is found, for example, in certain cult leaders, together with an equally aberrant submissiveness on the part of their willing victims. This psychology, when united with religion, can lead otherwise intelligent and educated people to utter self-destruction. Seemingly unbelievable accounts of this appear with fair regularity in the media, and in fact, the beautiful person who related this story to me concluded, when she had finally emancipated herself, that it was precisely this pathological psychology that had victimized her.

I was trapped in a failed marriage for twenty-seven years. I thought that my reason for staying was the children, but something else was at work, too. I got married at nineteen and knew from the start that it was a mistake. I eventually attained a high-level job in the mortgage department of a bank, but my husband never got a job at all. So we lived on what I earned, plus occasional help from his parents. Still, he dictated how that income was to be spent. Indeed, he dictated everything. His job was supposed to be to take care of the house, but he insisted that this should be up to the children. The result was that we lived in such filth that my parents finally refused to visit. I eventually made a room for myself, which I could keep clean, and that is where, in effect, I lived. There was no limit to my husband's control and, step by step, I let myself fall under it. I liked to use makeup, but he forbade it. He even decided what I could wear at work. I bought panty hose, as appropriate for the way I wanted to dress for work, but he made me return them, insisting that I wear socks, which made me look ridiculous. He would not allow a microwave oven in the house, insisting that it was useless and might even be dangerous. I needed closet rods for my clothes, rods that I could reach, but he demanded that they be set high, which meant that I had to find something to stand on to reach them. This, like so many of his demands, was entirely arbitrary, having nothing to do with him. He wouldn't let me buy diet soda, even for myself, until he eventually discovered that he liked it, too.

That is how we lived all those years, in complete disorder and dirt, and he neglected himself as well as the house. He was dirty and smelled bad. There was no love, never any real intimacy. Sex was always for his satisfaction, at times of his choosing. For me it was something to endure. The yard was as neglected as the house, and to make matters worse, he collected all kinds of animals—horses, turkeys, a cow, goats, ducks, sheep, even a peacock. In the house he kept fish. One of the horses died, of starvation, and lay in the yard for weeks.

I meanwhile became frightfully overweight, fighting depression by eating all the time. We tried counseling, but he was so abusive at our sessions that I gave up. Then he found a clergyman, who was not at all interested in helping with our problems, but wanted only to talk about his own marriage. He pretty much agreed with my husband's ideas, so we got nowhere with that.

It might seem that things could not get worse, but they did. He had decided on a trip to Florida for a vacation, and at just that time I had a miscarriage. I was bleeding all the way there, and yet, I was expected to do my share of the driving. We had a huge van, so big that I could hardly drive it. When we finally got there, I insisted on going to a hospital, because I was getting weaker and weaker, but he opposed it, out of fear that the doctors would perform a hysterectomy, thereby destroying his chance to father any more children. I finally did go, and he went, too, to make sure they performed no such surgery.

After we got back my life continued down hill. The board of health condemned our house as unfit for occupancy, because of the dirt, the neglected animals, and all, but with his parent's help my husband hired a lawyer and got that lifted. I was by that time crying all the time, until I could not open my eyes or go to work. I ended up in the emergency ward of the hospital, but nothing was done there to help me. I guess I was beyond help.

Finally, I just fled. That was five years ago, and I have been trying ever since to get a divorce, but he just keeps throwing up obstacles, so by now I wonder whether there is any point in pursuing it. At least I'm out of there.

That extreme kind of control is, of course, not common in our culture, but the need to control is common, at least on the part of husbands, and it almost always makes married love difficult, if not impossible. And since, according to the basic theme of this book, genuine marriage rests on married love and nothing else, then control is always to some extent incompatible with marriage, even in marriages that, to outward appearances, are "lasting." Wives once, by the force of custom, more or less accepted a degree of control by their husbands, but no longer. The forces of feminism, which men so often totally fail to understand, militate against it, and this is certainly part of the reason that so many marriages fail. The solution is not to attack feminism, as is fairly common, but to enter marriage with an understanding of what marriage is, and what it requires.

WHY MARRIAGE?

If the institution of marriage is in such a sorry state, why get married? You have only about a fifty-fifty chance of succeeding and, to make it worse, failure here can be disastrous. You would certainly pause before taking even the most alluring job if there was a similar likelihood of failure, and all the more so if failure would mean lasting poverty. Nor would you sign up for the most exciting cruise if you were warned that it was likely to end up in some dismal foreign port that you could escape from only at great expense. Why, then, do people embark upon the risky adventure of marriage?

The answer, of course, is that they are in love. We shall examine shortly just what that means, and how illusory it is as a portent of happiness. But meanwhile, let us consider whether there is any longer much point in getting married. It is generally thought that marriage is the only way of "tying the knot," that is, basing a lasting relationship on a secure foundation. That, too, is an illusion, as should by now be apparent.

Marriage, it would seem, is in fact becoming an anachronism. It is being replaced by cohabitation. Census figures show that cohabitation between the sexes almost doubled during a recent decade, while formal marriages increased by a paltry 7 percent. On top of this, marriagelike unions between persons of the same sex have become common and, except in some religious quarters, increasingly accepted. It has been estimated that there are now over five million unmarried couples living together.

Census figures also show a declining divorce rate. This has been hailed by some as proof that the institution of marriage is becoming stronger and, by implication, that marital unhappiness is declining. In fact, the figures indicate nothing of the kind, but are instead a reflection of the fact that cohabitation has been replacing marriage. Cohabiting couples need no divorce proceedings to break up; they simply go their separate ways, and thus escape statistical enumeration.

And that, by itself, is a strong argument for cohabitation rather than marriage. You avoid completely the cost and pain of getting a divorce in case things don't work out.

According to a *New York Times* article, published on March 24, 2002, in northern European countries fewer and fewer cohabiting couples are bothering to get married before having children, and little if any stigma now attaches to this. In Norway, according to recent figures, nearly half of all births were to unwed parents. Even in Roman Catholic France over 40 percent of the parents are unwed when their children are born, although most of these do get married eventually in order to protect their children's inheritance rights. Even socially and politically prominent people can cohabit, sometimes for years, with no loss of status. Norway has an unmarried member of parliament who became a mother when she was holding an important cabinet post and has continued raising her son on her own. In Ireland the prime minister makes no effort to conceal his de facto marriage, even though he has never been divorced from his first wife. In general, the welfare of children is deemed more important than any formalities of marriage, so the children of unmarried couples have by law the same protection as any others. In America, by contrast, about half of all unmarried mothers live in poverty.

But can cohabitation really be considered a substitute for marriage? If a man and a woman intend to spend their lives together, in strict fidelity to each other, to raise a family and so on, then should they not get married? The answer is not obvious, and what might work for some might not work for others. What is very clear is that the legalization of a marriage relationship does little for its stability, so that, contrary to what is so widely held, it is by itself no reason for it.

Not so long ago cohabitation between the sexes was totally unacceptable and immoral. It was considered adultery, pure and simple. It is still a crime in some jurisdictions, and while such statutes are not enforced, they are also not repealed, due to the influence of churches. Cohabiting couples are no longer banished from the professions, such as teaching, and are even accepted without censure in most churches.

Cohabiting couples, if they are serious, typically take upon themselves all the responsibilities and advantages of marriage, such as sexual fidelity, sharing of property, raising children, and so on. All that is missing is the formal legality. This has become so common that there have arisen strong advocates and a very active, nonprofit organization to promote it, called the Alternatives to Marriage Project. Indeed, there are liberal clergy willing to preside over a wedding, in a church, with guests, witnesses, flowers, reception, and everything. Such "services of commitment" are fairly common for same-sex couples, but a cohabiting man and woman can sometimes do the same. No marriage license needs to be obtained and no certificate of marriage is issued. The minister omits from the service the words "by the power vested in me by the state," but he *need not* omit the words "I now pronounce you man and wife." The wife can take the husband's surname if she wishes, and they can bestow that surname on any children born of the marriage. That will be the name on the birth certificates, and no question of legitimacy will ever arise. What the couple *cannot* do is use their relationship to defraud. But then, financial fraud is forbidden to everyone.

Such couples do not, then, need the permission of government to become what I shall call a de facto married couple. What is more important, they do not need such permission, in the form of a court proceeding, to dissolve the marriage. From a libertarian viewpoint this is of enormous importance, for the question can surely be asked what business government can possibly have in choices so private and personal as this.

It is in fact government itself that is partly responsible for the rise of de facto marriages, these being the unanticipated result of legal restrictions on the inheritance of pensions. A widow, for example, is entitled to the benefits from her deceased husband's social security, and, of course, vice versa. But what if she remarries? Should she still be entitled to those lifelong benefits? It was thought not. So a compromise was reached. If she remarries before age sixty (fifty-five in the case of civil service pensions), then she forfeits those benefits forever, but if she remarries even one day after that age, then they will continue for life. This is obviously arbitrary. It was apparently assumed that no one would want to marry someone that old. The effect, however, was to place many widows under that age in a bind. Should they give up their pension rights or abandon hope of remarriage? So they compromised. They entered into de facto marriages, and over time this became almost totally accepted. The sense of guilt that some such couples felt soon passed, and the customary legal documentation of marriage was seen to be for most practical purposes meaningless.

From this, of course, it was but a short step to the acceptance of de facto marriage at any age. College deans no longer take much notice of male and female students living together in dormitories. Many men and women just out of college and starting professional training enter into such relationships without stirring the least disapproval, even from their parents.

In fact, cohabitation is fast becoming the normal route to formal marriage. Couples try living together, often for a considerable time, before tying the knot. This is in some ways very strange, for one can wonder why, if the de facto marriage has proved fulfilling and durable, they should then bother with the legality and an often expensive and elaborate wedding. It is probably due in part to the force of custom. People imagine that there can be no real commitment without a wedding.

Of course there are sometimes reasons, having nothing to do with ethics or custom, for making everything legal. Laws governing marriage, besides imposing restrictions, also create benefits that are sometimes considerable. Let us, then, compare formal and de facto marriages with respect to these.

The blessings traditionally associated with marriage are such things as ongoing love and emotional support, the defeat of loneliness, security, home life, sexual exclusivity, the opportunity to raise children together, the sharing property, and so on. These can flourish no less in a de facto marriage. Couples who represent themselves to the world as married are accepted as such. They are never asked to prove it. Employers raise no doubts, and even insurance companies and government agencies usually take their word for it.

The disadvantages of such an arrangement are that its partners cannot file a joint income tax return or obtain family coverage for health insurance without risking a charge of criminal fraud. There is, however, usually little if any advantage in filing joint tax returns, and usually either partner can include the children in his or her health insurance.

What, then, about security? It is sometimes supposed that, without a binding legal marriage, one or the other partner, or perhaps both, has only a fragile security. A "marriage" that rests only on mutual agreement, it is thought, is no real marriage and can be casually dissolved. The female partner is especially likely to feel such insecurity, and badger her partner to marry her, even after years of cohabitation. Men usually feel less threatened.

There is some truth in this, which we shall examine shortly, but first we must ask: Just how strong is the bond of legal marriage?

Actually, the bond is not very strong at all. The legality of the arrangement binds nothing. Half of such legally "binding" marriages end in divorce. How tight can the knot have been if that is the result? A marriage is not made secure by the filing of documents, and certainly not by vows, however solemnly uttered. Marriage vows, it turns out, are binding only so long as the marriage lasts. Its actual strength can rest on nothing but the unshakable love of its partners, which can flourish and grow in a de facto marriage no less than in a traditional one. Indeed, it may be even stronger, since no one is likely to feel trapped, and thus resentful, in a marriage that is kept alive and vibrant by the devotion and consideration of both partners.

A formal marriage is typically launched in a church or synagogue, sometimes with an elaborate ceremony presided over by a clergyperson. This gives an aura of sanctity and seriousness to the step being taken, but it adds nothing to the durability of the marriage. The tireless promotion of traditional marriage by conservative religionists and politicians is largely hollow. Religious people are just as susceptible to friction, frustration, and deep unhappiness in marriage as anyone else. In fact, according to one study, the rate of divorce in the so-called Bible Belt considerably *exceeds* the average (*New York Times*, May 21, 2001). So much for the claim that those who pray together stay together.

There is, however, likely to be a real threat to economic security in a de facto marriage that fails. A judge is likely to view the female partner in such a relationship as only a willing mistress without any claim to her partner's property. Moreover, courts are increasingly taking the position that marriage is a true partnership, like any other, in which the partners are to be treated as equals whatever might be their different roles. This means that, in case the marriage is dissolved, property will be divided equitably. Exceptions are made only for such things as pensions in which one partner has invested prior to the marriage, tangible and intangible property that was inherited, and so on—in other words, property that was gained entirely outside the marriage. Once married, however, husband and wife are considered to have contributed equally to whatever is accumulated, even if the income that produced it was in fact earned exclusively by only one of them. If, for example, a wife's role was to manage the household, and the husband's to provide the income, then it is assumed that the resulting property belongs equally to both.

This view of marriage was driven home by a New York appellate court in a case in which the wife was the wage earner while her husband was in medical school. Soon after he finished his training and entered into a lucrative practice he sued for divorce. The court took the view that his medical degree was, in effect, a license to earn money, and that the wife had toiled just as hard to get it by supporting him through those years. She was, accordingly, awarded a large portion of his entire *future* income.

In another case a wealthy business executive filed for divorce, offering his wife one million dollars as a final settlement. She attracted a great deal of media attention by demanding ten million. She did not get all that, but the court did award her most of it, the view being that she had earned it, just by being his wife.

Finally, in a third case, a man left his wife, without formally divorcing her, and entered into a lasting de facto marriage with someone else. Years later, when he died, a court awarded the first wife one-third of his estate and gave nothing to the de facto wife, noting that the second marriage was without legal validity.

This being the trend, we can expect that partners, and especially men, are increasingly likely to prefer de facto marriages rather than confront the possibility of someday being at the mercy of a court. Women, on the other hand, are more likely to seek the financial security of legal marriage.

But need this be true? Can de facto marriage provide the same security while avoiding the pitfalls of formal marriage?

It can go a long way. A de facto married couple can, for example, put all their property in joint ownership from the start. That, once done, settles for good the question of who owns what. They can also make a joint will, each naming the other as legatee, and such that the will can be modified only with the concurrence of both. They can establish trusts, execute proxies, and bestow powers of attorney on each other such that both can act in the other's behalf in any matters of property, name each other as beneficiaries of life insurance, and so on. Real estate, cars, and the like can be in joint ownership. If you own title to something, then it cannot be taken from you. And finally, a couple can, without formal marriage, execute a legally binding marriage covenant to cover any matter of security important to either, although this, unlike the other steps outlined, would be seen by many to cast doubt upon the love that they believe to be the basis of their relationship.

We can conclude, then, that the legalization of a marriage relationship has little to be said in its favor and much to be said against it. But perhaps most significant of all, de facto marriage has become so generally accepted, ethically, socially, and in every other way, that one can, indeed, wonder whether traditional marriage still has any significant value at all.

chapter 2

ceremonies, vows, and the meaning of marriage

COURTSHIP

There are many reasons why so many marriages fail, but if we had to pick one, it would probably be courtship.

Of course courtship in its original sense is archaic. A man no longer "courts" a woman, eventually getting around to "popping the question" or asking her father for her hand, and the image of a man on bended knee is laughable. But this only means that courtship has changed, and so far as marital stability is concerned, it certainly has not changed for the better.

Courtship is now extended flirtation, on the part of both sexes. Each tries to look his or her best. Faults are concealed. The whole idea is simply to win over the other. There is a great deal of affection expressed physically, and increasingly, much sex. The whole process is likely to be exhilarating beyond description, and the two see themselves, and are seen by others, as "in love." A man in this role is eager to appear *strong* in every way possible—possessed of great sexual vigor, command over others, successful in whatever he undertakes, and so on—while a woman is likely to be more concerned with feeling attractive and desired. There is, in short, a great deal of acting or role-playing, to the extent that neither really comes to know the other. If shortcomings are detected—if the man is a bit sloppy, for example, or the woman perhaps extravagant—then it is thought that love will overcome these little things and that the two will settle into warm and loving harmony.

The very language used to describe courtship conveys its utter mindlessness. The two are said to be "madly in love," or "head over heels," to have "fallen" into this state, to be "crazy" about each other, and so on—all of these expressions suggesting a total lack of control. Reason and intelligence have been set aside, giving way to passion. It is all very heady, but the consequences are likely to be those that always accompany irrational behavior, namely, chaos or even disaster.

What is wrong with all this, of course, is that neither really gets to know the other. Neither is quite what the other seems to see. Every effort has been made to insure this. The goal from the beginning has been to *win over* the other, to appear at one's best rather than to appear as one actually is.

And yet, as soon as the two have settled into marriage, each is confronted with what the other *actually* is. There is no longer any need to pretend, to cover anything over, for the objective of the courtship has been achieved—to win the other over or, what almost amounts to the same thing, to gain possession. Now, finally, each can revert to his or her true self without risk. Indeed, there is no choice in this, for two people cannot be married and making a life together very long without penetrating the artificiality that has ruled until then, and actually coming to know each other for the reality that is there.

Sometimes this happens very quickly. A man who budgets his

time, trying to make every hour count, soon finds that his bride can waste hours on some frivolous thing, like a crossword puzzle or gossiping with a friend on the telephone. A woman who prizes neatness, cleanliness, and order quickly discovers that her husband does not bathe frequently, goes unshaven, and leaves dirty clothes about. A man scrupulous about expenditures finds himself married to an extravagant woman, who buys unneeded things on impulse, and so on. The possibilities for friction, which have until marriage been kept carefully in the background, are limitless.

It is no wonder that marriages fail. Those who get married are very likely not to really know whom they are marrying, and find themselves in for bitter surprises.

One can imagine an intelligent alternative to this madness, but it is unlikely to become the accepted pattern, except, perhaps, for some of those who have been burned, that is, who have suffered the emotional and tangible costs of divorce, maybe more than once. This alternative would be, quite simply, for couples seeking marriage to be totally and candidly themselves, without pretense, and truly, for better or for worse. Let each see what he or she is actually getting. This would require total openness with respect to everything. Each, for example, should disclose any health problems. Both should describe honestly how they feel about everything that will arise in a marriage, such as religion, children, sex, tastes in music, food, money, travel, hobbies—everything, however seemingly insignificant. Even small things, such as how one uses time, can become a source of ongoing irritation or rewarding companionship. And above all, both should be totally open about finances, that is, income, inheritances, who shall be considered to own what, and so on.

Indeed, if people were really rational, then government itself would insist, by statute, that couples contemplating marriage must not only supply to each other an inventory of attitudes on all such things, but also that they actually live together for a certain minimum time—say, six months—before any marriage license could be granted. If the foundation for any governmental interest in marriage is the reduction of divorce and the protection of children, then something like this would clearly be a step in the right direction.

But there is, of course, no likelihood whatsoever that anything like this will ever become public policy. People will go right on falling in love, abandoning reason, opening the doors to the misery that produces costly and painful divorce. Meanwhile, government, while setting conditions for permission to divorce, will, as now, require little more than evidence that the couple do not have a venereal disease and are not drunk when they take the marital vows.

The following account, very atypical, is a refreshing contrast to romantic courtship:

My courtship of Mary, if it can be called that, was for several weeks a long-distance one. I was the veteran of three failed marriages and certainly didn't want to risk another. At the same time, I could not stand being alone. My days and nights of loneliness were terrible, and I was becoming a zombie. I heard about Mary through a friend, who told me she was, of recent date, a widow. I got in touch with her, and letters were soon followed by daily, and sometimes twice daily, phone calls. I was falling in love again, sight unseen this time. What was the chance of this working? Not much, if I thought about it, but my hopes soared. So I got on a plane and flew off to meet her. My palms were sweating as the plane began to descend, as I knew we were about to lay eyes on each other for the first time. The uncertainty, combined with the desperate need and hope, were overwhelming. The doubts melted in minutes when we met. She was calm, poised, and totally lovely. We went off to her beautiful house, talked easily about insignificant things, dined out, and then, in the darkness of her hallway, I asked if she was as lonely as I. She was. We spent that night in the same bed, but without intimacy; I was not ready for that, nor was she. It was wonderfully pleasant, and reassuring; neither of us expected anything except considerateness, neither tried to impress.

That was a brief and reassuring encounter. I was pretty sure my loneliness was over, but still, we didn't know much about each other, even though neither had tried to withhold anything. So I flew down again, and this time I set about to disclose absolutely everything about myself, to pretend nothing, and, at my initiative, she did the same. In a lengthy discussion we compared our feelings and beliefs on everything we could think of: money, children, sex, music, politics, hobbies, pets, nature, social life, travel, books, religion, food—absolutely everything. We got to know each other, for just what we are, not for how we want to appear. I had even taken with me my income tax returns, not to impress her, for there was nothing in them to impress anyone, but just so she could see that I was secure, though not rich.

Her next step was to come visit me, meet my young children and see my situation. Romance, in the usual sense, was still kept in the background. The time was for learning, not courting, in the usual sense.

Then she flew back home, sold all her furniture, put her house on the market, and moved in with me. That was ten years ago, and they have been the happiest years either of us has ever known. I cannot imagine anything that could unsettle this marriage. We seem to read each other's minds. We are in love—not like you see in films, but it is deep, comfortable, reassuring, constant, and indestructible.

Again one wishes, in the light of that account, that some law could be passed requiring all couples contemplating marriage to go through some sort of process of self-disclosure. But of course nothing like that is ever going to happen. Sometimes clergypersons will insist on some sort of premarital counseling, as a condition of presiding at the wedding, and that is certainly a step in the right direction. On the whole, however, we all prefer to stare enviously at the couple whose only reason for getting married is that they are *in love*. This, somehow, is held up as an ideal, the appropriate prelude to the most difficult and hazard-strewn relationship that two people can undertake. The result? Half of all marriages collapse into bitterness and fail, and most of those that manage to survive limp along, beset with unmet expectations and often deep unhappiness.

THE WEDDING

It would be difficult to imagine a less suitable way of entering into marriage than by the classic American wedding, and yet, somehow, the very opposite is widely assumed.

By the classic wedding is meant the familiar grand ceremony. A date is picked and plans are made for months, sometimes years, in advance. A clergyperson presides, usually in a holy place of some kind, surrounded by flowers, and in front of an audience, often large. The bride approaches slowly from the back, on the elbow of her father (who is there to "give her away," and who will often be paying the gargantuan costs), she joins the groom at the altar, and the solemn recital of vows follows. The atmosphere is one of great joy and emotion, often with tears on the part of some of the female witnesses. There then follows the reception, sometimes dancing, and at last, the nuptial flight when, it was once supposed, the marriage is consummated.

All this is preceded, of course, by vast preparations. The costly bridal gown will of course be worn only once, unless it happens to be a treasured heirloom or preserved to become one. Weeks are spent creating it. Special witnesses are chosen—bridesmaids and a "best man." Photographers are hired, and the photographs preserved in a special album and/or some electronic repository to be treasured forever. Sometimes, depending upon the celebrity or wealth of the families, news coverage will be provided. All this requires minute planning, from the selection of scriptural or inspirational passages to be read, the food to be served at the reception, the design of the wedding invitations, the list of those to be invited, and the location of the ceremony. In case this latter is not the regular place of worship of the bride, but is instead a secular hall, reservations must be made, sometimes far in advance. Postponement of the wedding can last for months or years in order to ensure that this place, perhaps coveted by others, will be available, and in at least one case a prospective bride reserved a hall three years in advance, *before* she had any idea who the groom would be.

Of course not all weddings are like this. Couples are sometimes casually joined in marriage by a justice of the peace, who may until then have been unknown to them, and in some jurisdictions they can become married simply through cohabitation for a set time, the familiar "common-law" marriage.

But what has been described is the classic wedding, and all the energy, cost, and planning that goes into it are somehow thought to contribute to the happiness and stability of the marriage thus entered into. It seems the surest way of "tying the knot," so that it will stay tied.

But what is thus thought of as the most important day in the life of the bride is likely to turn out to have been a disaster. There is absolutely nothing in such a ceremony that will contribute to the happiness and stability of the marriage thus begun. On the contrary, everything there is a distraction from what is really essential to successful marriage. Instead of the principals, bride and groom, seeing each other for what they are, the opposite is what is promoted. They see each other bathed in glamour and beauty, all of it artificially created. They see each other for what they are not.

When the frenzy of the wedding is over and the newlyweds begin to come back to earth, then the factors that will contribute to a long and stable marriage, or those that will tend to undermine it, begin to emerge. Pretense is over. Each begins to revert to his or her true self. Perhaps the bride will find a husband as considerate and solicitous as the man she fell in love with, but, more likely, he turns out to be somewhat less than this. He has won her, and further effort in that direction is no longer in order. Now perhaps she sees a man increasingly prone to take her for granted, or, as so often happens, one who is controlling. He, too, sees a woman who is starting to emerge from the one he knew, maybe someone devoted and interested in things that are important to him, but maybe not. Perhaps he finds a streak of hitherto unsuspected silliness, or a woman with a vast capacity for wasting her time on frivolous things. Or he finds an independent strong-willed woman who challenges him, and he sees this as a threat. The possibilities are endless.

The classic wedding portends none of this. The wedding was all show and pretense. This is reality. The wedding was but for a few brief moments. This is supposed to be forever. And what the wedding really accomplished was to divert attention from the reality that counts. Bride and groom solemnly promise love and fidelity for life, but nothing in those vows can prevent their true personalities from emerging, often as a bitter surprise to one or both.

The first thing, of course, is for the love birds to realize that a wedding has very little to do with being married, and will very likely have a negative effect. No knot can be tied by the ceremony, but only by the personalities of those thus joined together.

And, on the more practical level, persons contemplating marriage should by all means actually live together, as if married, for a considerable time before formal marriage takes place. Let them face together the daily challenges and annoyances of life and the outside pressures, such as bills to be paid. That is the test. Then, if the relationship survives all this intact, the two can get married with some assurance that it will work. It is this sort of thing, and not ceremony and vows, that ties the knot. If stability of marriage is the goal, then a pretrial of it is probably the surest way of achieving it. It is, in any case, vastly better than all the make-believe embodied in the classic wedding.

THE SECOND TIME AROUND

Second marriages are more unstable than the first ones, if divorce rate is a measure of stability. This does not mean that divorced people should not remarry. It means that they should be on guard.

First-time partners are usually not on guard at all. They are too much in love, and if problems are staring them in the face, they prefer not to acknowledge them, assuming that love will overcome everything. The thought that they should take some time to discuss finances, spending habits, even such basic considerations as religious attitudes, seems to them to cast doubt on the power of love.

The thought of composing a prenuptial agreement is to most such couples out of the question.

Of course these attitudes are bound to breed problems in second marriages, and probably most second-timers are at least somewhat aware of this.

The special problems of persons entering second marriages are apt to be, first, children. If one of the partners brings children to the relationship, especially adolescents, then a whole new set of relationships challenges them. This is especially true if the partner is the custodial parent. Adolescents appraise the new partner, and the appraisal is very likely to be poor, the more so if those children have a powerful attachment to the parent left behind. This makes any kind of rapport, to say nothing of genuine affection, difficult for the stepparent. And the problem of children is enormously magnified in the case of a "blended" family, that is, one in which both parents bring children to the new relationship. The integration of them all can be difficult to the point of impossibility. Rationally, the children should be accepting of the new marriage, even enthusiastically embrace it, but children are seldom rational. Jealousies, and competition for the attention and affection of the original parent, inevitably arise.

Even apart from children, there are special reasons for the lesser stability of second marriages. For example, a divorced person is very likely to feel that he or she has been put down, abandoned, and made to feel inadequate by the divorced partner. There is, then, a strong need to remarry, just in order to reestablish self-respect and prove something to the world. And this can impel one to rush into a marriage with an unsuitable partner.

And finally, having been through divorce once, persons marrying for the second time are apt not to be so fearful of it. They've been there before.

The way to overcome these problems is through total communication. Thus, before the fateful step is taken, the couple should go over, exhaustively, all of their likes and dislikes and attitudes; for example, how each of them feels about: religion, sex, children, money, saving and spending, holidays, food, music, animals, books, films, travel, how they spend their time, politics—whatever they can dig up to talk about. Any of these can be a stumbling block, large or small. For example, if one has a fixed practice of frugality, and the other gives saving money a very low priority, then the potentiality for trouble is enormous. And so with all the other things, to a greater or lesser degree.

Ideally, of course, newlyweds would do this, too, but there is little likelihood that many ever will. Such a discussion just puts a damper on the love that is driving them into marriage. Romance is intoxicating, this sort of thing is not. And there, in a nutshell, is why so many marriages end in divorce, and why so many of those that do not are unfulfilling to the point of being miserable.

PRENUPTIAL AGREEMENTS

The clash of reason and romance is displayed with perfect clarity in the idea of a prenuptial agreement. Sometimes such agreements are mainly concerned with how a couple envision the marriage they are about to enter into, that is, who will do what, how responsibilities will be divided, and so on. If, for example, both work, then how will housework be divided? Will total family income be pooled, or will financial responsibilities be separated? Perhaps one will be in charge of investments, for example, another responsible for payment of bills, and so on.

That approach to the cooperation that every marriage rests upon is perfectly rational and need not evoke strong feelings of doubt or resentment, since no doubt is raised concerning the stability of the marriage itself. To formalize such an agreement in writing, however, is both superfluous and pointless, because there is no way of enforcing it. No attorney or court is interested in any dispute about who does the cooking or who feeds the dog. Moreover, such issues can easily be resolved by simple discussion. To put them in writing is only to cast doubt on a partner's trustworthiness. Once the marriage has been entered into, a simple reminder ("Remember, you said you were going to walk the dog") is perfectly adequate. To reduce such understandings to writing would be simply petty.

The matter is quite different, however, when it comes to property, and when the question is raised of how this will be divided up in the event that the marriage fails. Here the passion of love and the voice of reason simply collide, and there is no way of reconciling them. A couple approaching their wedding—a wedding that has, perhaps, been long planned, and for which elaborate and expensive preparations have been made—can hardly talk comfortably about a prenuptial agreement, which is clearly based on the premise that the marriage will fail. "I love you, forever and with all my heart," simply cannot be combined with "What do I get to keep if we get divorced?" All marriages are entered into with the romantic expectation of everlasting love and happiness, notwithstanding the realities. This may be known by both as the day of the wedding approaches, but, still, they would not be planning marriage if they were not convinced that it was going to be different. Nothing destroys rational thought as effectively as being in love.

This is why prenuptial agreements will never be popular in our culture. Where the issue is most likely to come up is with second (or third, etc.) marriages, and also, when one or the other is very rich.

People entering upon second marriages, for example, have tasted failure and therefore know the pitfalls. If earlier marriages broke up with great bitterness, then there is a strong incentive not to risk that again. Previously married people are, moreover, likely to be less driven by romantic impulse, even when the love is genuine and deep. They have been through it all before, and are likely to have realistic views without necessarily having become cynical.

Second marriages are also likely to involve children, perhaps on both sides. How the two families are to be integrated and provided for are matters of such importance, and often of such difficulty, that a written understanding might be needed—something setting forth what is understood to be the role of the stepparent, what the relationship with ex-spouses shall be, and so on.

Still, matters of that sort are best dealt with by candid discussion rather than formal agreement. Children, moreover, will have their own ways of dealing with the new relationships resulting from the blended families, and no agreements between parents, whether formal or informal, will have much effect on these.

The only time a formal, legally valid prenuptial agreement may be needed is when wealth is involved. If, for example, the bride's family is rich, and the money has been in the family for some time, back through generations, then her parents might badly want or even insist upon a prenuptial agreement. This is likely to stir deep resentment in the groom. It will seem to him that he is being assigned a second-class status, and that his bride, notwithstanding her professions of undying love, is really only seeking to rent him. There is clearly no risk in what is genuinely an indestructible union, and to raise questions concerning property rights, questions that are based on the supposition that the marriage will not last, is to betray a contradiction in one's intentions and expectations. It seems to amount to incorporating divorce rights into a marriage that rests on vows of permanence that will end only in death.

If we were governed by reason and intelligence rather than romantic fictions, then a prenuptial agreement would be made a legal precondition for issuing a marriage license, just as in some jurisdictions, sobriety and medical proof of freedom from sexually transmitted disease are required. This would remove any misgivings either partner might otherwise have about the other's sincerity. It would be simply a minor bureaucratic requirement, without any meaning in the case of a marriage that was in fact lasting, but of enormous importance in the case of the marital failure that, although neither partner wants to contemplate it, is a very real possibility, or even a strong likelihood. This would preclude the demeaning fighting over property and custody rights and much of the bitterness that accompanies divorce proceedings. Those emotion-laden matters would all have been settled in advance; perhaps not settled exactly as the divorcing couple would like, but settled, nevertheless, and almost certainly more intelligently, and with less pain and cost, than what would have resulted from extended and bitterly fought litigation.

This idea of making a prenuptial agreement a precondition of marriage, however reasonable it might seem, will never be put into effect. Partners contemplating marriage would simply draw up such an agreement without seriousness, and if it were provided by any judicial authority according to set formula, then it would not survive later challenge in court. Partners wanting out of a marriage could always exercise their right to disavow such an agreement, as not reflecting present realities, and no court would compel them to do otherwise.

So why suggest such a thing? To remind people, once again, that even with the best intentions and motives on the part of partners, marriage is a fragile thing. Vows, "till death do us part," have no real meaning when they can be so easily disregarded. Marital vows should be thought of as no more than poetic accompaniment to a wedding. For vows that have meaning, couples should set aside their romantic feelings long enough to draw up a prenuptial agreement, preferably with the help of an attorney. We should think of such an agreement as comparable to a will. No one likes to contemplate his or her own death, yet we know it is inevitable, and that a last will and testament is therefore a practical necessity. Since we know that divorce, though not inevitable, is a huge possibility, however auspicious the start of a marriage, we should apply the same thinking to prenuptial agreements.

THE MEANING OF MARRIAGE

Being married cannot, as we have seen, be simply a matter of having fulfilled certain ceremonial and legal formulas—wedding, duly authenticated certification, and so on. This may be what the law looks at, but if marriage is thought of in ethical terms, then it has to have a meaning deeper than this. Not everything that passes the tests of legality fulfills the requirements of ethics.

What is essential to being married, it is now claimed, is not anything readily seen, but rather a strong bond of love between its partners that is lasting and gives meaning to the idea of lifelong commitment. It is this *alone* that gives rise to every moral consideration involving the behavior of its partners. Infidelity, for example, is not merely the breach of some vow, but behavior that destroys the bond of love uniting man and wife. When that bond of love is gone, then the marriage is dead, even though no steps have been taken to end it, and a dead marriage is not a marriage at all. The fact that two people can continue to share the same roof in a loveless association does not mean that they are still married. They expected their love to be lasting, and it was not. When it died, the marriage died with it. If a woman or a man marries *just* to gain instant American citizenship, then they are not really married even if their union is never challenged. And it is the same for a man or a woman who marries *just* in order to get his or her hands on the spouse's wealth, even in cases where the legality of the relationship is not in dispute.

One should not say of unions in which the bond of love has been broken, or in which it never really existed, that these are not "good" marriages. They are not marriages at all, no matter what the legalities. Of course the laws governing marriage are often important, since they can govern certain matters of the utmost importance, such as custody of children, transfer of property, inheritance of pensions, and so on. Still, they have no relevance whatever to marriage as we are defining it here.

The consequences of thinking of marriage in ethical rather than merely legal terms can be far reaching. If, taking the legalistic approach, you define married partners' obligations to each other in terms of their marriage vows, then fidelity will have a very different and narrower meaning than if you define them in ethical terms, and you will also be on very weak ground because marriage vows seem to have no effect whatsoever on behavior. They are forgotten the moment an inducement to ignore them arises. Probably no one, for example, has been restrained from adultery by thinking back to those vows, whereas genuine love for someone is a powerful force indeed. A couple who have drifted so far apart that they have not even seen each other for years, and give no thought to each other, cannot be described as *still married,* nor can either be any more unfaithful to the other than any other strangers. Ethically, they owe each other no more, but of course no less, than they owe to the next stranger who comes down the street.

We have here been alluding to "the bond of love," as if this were a perfectly clear idea that is known to all. Of course it is not clear at all. "Love" is a word that is tossed around so much, with so many meanings, and more often than not simply trivialized, as to be virtually meaningless. Parents love their children, patriots love their country, a philanderer loves women, some people love bird watching, others motor cars, and so on. The word means different things in each of these contexts, and when we speak of the bond of love as the foundation of true marriage, we are obviously not using the term in any of these senses. The deeper meaning has yet to be explored.

Another good reason for defining marriage in ethical rather than legal terms is that it enables us to treat the so-called civil unions of partners of the same sex the same as those of the heterosexual unions that we dignify as marriages. Such unions are rarely treated as marriages under the law or even by churches, notwithstanding the fact that they fulfill all the ethical foundations of marriage. Surely the concept of infidelity, for example, applies to such couples no less than others. Betrayal is not a concept that is defined in terms of gender. And even the law in most jurisdictions recognize that homosexual couples can adopt children, that the laws relating to spousal abuse apply, and so on. Legally such people are not married, but ethically they clearly are.

It is not uncommon for people, imagining that they are expressing an ethical ideal, to speak of marriage as a *commitment*, and even, sometimes, as a *contract*. Marriages that have lasted, in the sense of not ending in divorce, are sometimes described this way, its partners finding in this notion a source of pride. They have stuck it out, done their duty to their children, forsaken all others, and so on—in short, they have honored their vows.

Of course there is nothing really wrong with this, and partners who take comfort in this way of looking at things are hardly to be dismissed. Even the clergy tend to talk this way. Couples, when they got married, made certain promises to each other, and they kept them and deserve praise. The fact that the most important promise of all—the promise of love—has not been fulfilled, except in some narrow and negative sense, does not matter, for this, after all, is not something that can be promised anyway. No one can guarantee what his feelings are going to be over the years.

Still, it needs to be stressed that, while marriage does indeed involve commitment, this is not the noblest of ethical ideals, and the concept of *contract* is even less so.

Commitment and contract are basically concepts of finance, and what they presuppose is pure self-interest. When someone commits himself to certain terms, then it is presupposed that he does so for advantage; he expects to get something from it, in return for something that is given. Institutions such as banks enter into commitments with persons seeking loans or whatever, as well as with other institutions, and even nations enter into commitments with each other, through treaties and the like. Contracts rest upon the same presuppositions; contractual arrangements are entered into for the sake of mutual advantage. And there is surely nothing wrong with this. Social life would be quite impossible without such mutual commitments, the very minimum of which would amount to saying, "I will help you if you will help me." And furthermore, marriage, as so conceived, is an extremely useful thing in fostering social stability.

What is missing in this view, however, is any genuinely ethical factor. All the conditions of commitment or contract can be met in a relationship that is totally devoid of love, and it can hardly be claimed that acting from self-interest or even from scrupulous fidelity to rules is superior to acting from love. Moreover, putting it the other way around, when partners are united in abiding love, then all of the obligations of commitment are automatically met.

None of this is meant to imply that partners who keep their marriage intact for life, perhaps from no higher incentive than adherence to the vows they long ago exchanged, have nothing to be proud of. What they cannot claim, however, is a truly successful marriage. Indeed, from the standpoint of ethics they are not really married at all.

The following account, of an elderly New England couple, illustrates what is, and what is not, admirable about lifetime commitment:

> My sister and I never thought that Mom and Dad had much of anything in common beyond the interest that they took in us while we were growing up. They hardly ever did anything together, except sometimes go visit some relative. He had his friends, and she hers, and their interests were about as far apart as any could be. They even lived, more or less, in different parts of the house. Dad had his shop and his gardening and a room that was thought of as his where he read his magazines, and Mom had her church work. We never saw them get really angry with each other, except for little annoyances, but then, they never expressed much feeling of any kind.
>
> We realized one day that their golden wedding anniversary was coming up. Neither of them had said a thing about it, but we decided to do something for them, as a surprise. We invited about thirty people to come over, swearing them to secrecy, and arranged for food and refreshments for a party on the lawn. We even paid a couple to come play the guitar and sing.
>
> It was a huge success. The local newspaper even came and took pictures. Dad got all dressed up, and at the end when

everyone was leaving, there the two stood, on the porch, holding hands, and Dad was smiling—something he did not do very often. I'm sure they were happy that day, and proud, too.

Yes, but proud of what? Not, certainly, of the wonderful marriage they had created together. What they had done was fulfill their commitment to each other, a commitment they had made a half-century ago, and raise their children. There is something to admire in this, but it is not the fulfillment of any ideal of marriage.

LOVE AND THE SENSE OF SELF-WORTH

The picture of marriage that was presented earlier may appear negative, even cynical. Now it is time to recall what was said at the outset; namely, that no happiness exceeds the happiness that can be found in marriage. This cannot, of course, be proved, but the truth of it can hopefully be illustrated.

What we are talking about now is what I have been calling *true marriage,* that is, marriage that rests on undying love and not on human artificialities. The earlier discussion, accordingly, centered upon those artificialities—courtship, weddings, romantic love, and so on. To portray these in a negative way is not to portray marriage itself that way—unless, of course, you still insist on thinking of marriage as a relationship based upon weddings, legalities, vows, commitment, or some imagined contract. What I have tried to show is that marriage cannot really rest upon such things as these. There is a far better way to think about marriage and, once thought of in this way, its power to generate profound happiness becomes obvious.

True marriage is based upon enduring love. But what is that? It is astonishing how little this concept is understood. The mere utterance of the word seems to be an invitation to depart from reality.

Love, as it is thought of here, is clearly a concept of psychology, and not a very mysterious one. It rests on a fact of human psychology that is at once common to all, seemingly banal, and nevertheless almost never seriously discussed. That fact is the sense of self-worth. This is the truly universal incentive, the prism through which we view all of our relationships with others. Even things to which we give little or no thought reflect it—our speech, the way we walk, dress, everything. Belittle a person, ever so mildly, and you create automatic enmity. Reinforce a person's sense of self-worth, ever so mildly, and you establish trust, friendship. Be totally aware of it, all the time, in someone you care deeply about, and you nourish the most powerful of human forces, which is love. True love is best seen, then, not in its dramatic expressions, which are the substance of love poems and stories, but in the most banal, everyday experiences.

If you diminish, even slightly, someone's sense of self-worth, then the hurt is lasting, and indeed, often never forgotten. The put-downs you received as a child are remembered forever. If a parent or relative spoke slightingly of one of your achievements, however small, it is likely never to be forgotten. The same is true of your failures, even those that you know are of no lasting significance, in case they were rubbed in by some adult. A father who routinely belittles his son is simply cruel. The wounds never heal. You remember with discomfort the day your teacher humiliated you before your friends, and if you think of that teacher decades later, that is the first thing that comes to your mind. If, in your first adolescent love, you were belittled by the object of that love, then again, you are scarred forever, even though you imagine that you have long since put it out of your mind. If she commented on your clumsiness as a dancer, or your ineptitude in attempts at affection, or mocked some less than intelligent remark, then these insignificant things stand and the hurt remains, even though buried.

Consider further why high-powered executives are so driven, to the point sometimes of neglecting their health, their families, and what would seem to be the very ingredients of happiness. It is not for the resulting wealth, for that already exceeds their needs, and is, in any case, to them but another token of their self-worth.

An author or poet craves glowing reviews and large audiences more than the publisher's royalties. Scholars who never expect to reach significant audiences are rewarded simply by seeing their works in print.

Employers, too, are coming to appreciate the motivating force of this factor. They have not always. The assumption used to be, and to a large extent still is, that an employee's basic interest is compensation, when what he or she wants most is recognition. Studies have shown that companies whose personnel policies recognize this consistently do better than others. Such a company encourages its employees—very likely called associates—to participate in planning; provides them with partial, though trivial, ownership; and invites them to important meetings with management, where the highest officers of the company are outwardly indistinguishable from the rest. The focus, in short, is not on wages, but on what is far more important, the sense of self-worth.

This description could go on and on, but these somewhat random observations should be enough to bring the idea of self-worth clearly before us. And in this concept we can find the basis, not only for married love, but for all genuine love—but not, of course, the familiar love that is identified with attraction, or with possession. These are in fact antithetical to what we are describing.

Thus, a man does not express love for his wife by showing her off for her beauty, as if she were some kind of trophy, nor by showering her with gifts. Behavior like this is usually the expression of a man's love for himself, not for her. Nor is it an expression of love to leave a tender note on the refrigerator for her to find, or by remembering to bring her a rose on Valentine's Day. This sort of thing is prompted by all kinds of motives, often by nothing more than a desire to impress, which is again, *self-love*. A father does not express love for his son by trying to mold him to some preconceived model, such as that of a star athlete, but by constant awareness of whatever he has done well, whether it be large or small. So it is, too, with friends, associates, strangers, even those one dislikes.

People whose lives and work seem to be of little significance do not think of themselves that way. A man whose work consists of nothing more demanding than delivering mail takes pride in doing it well. He may envy the rich or powerful, but his sense of self-worth would not be enhanced if he were to change places with them, for it is already the most powerful force in his life.

So you enrich a person's life just by being aware of him, of his needs, his self-doubts, his sensitivities. And this awareness provides the basis not only for friendship and even love, but also for injury. You know how to wound, and if you are capable of love, then you refrain—even when such injury is "deserved."

Here, then, we can see the real foundation of fulfilling marriage, as well as the reason that so many marriages die, often to the point of ending in divorce.

Our obligations to our partners in marriage are not created by laws, customs, or vows, except in the most minimal sense. They instead rest upon the most basic obligation of all, which is, *to be aware* of your wife or husband from moment to moment, aware of his or her sensitivities, the things that hurt, however subtly, and the things that evoke the sense of warmth.

MARRIED LOVE

We have said married love is the foundation of marriage, considered in its true sense as a relationship that is lasting and deeply rewarding. This is to distinguish it from what is usually, and trivially, thought of as marriage; namely, a status conferred by the ceremony of wedding. It is likewise distinguished from all those things that are popularly referred to as love, such as someone's love for bird watching, or sailing, or whatever, or even more commonly, the release of adrenaline experienced by young lovers, sometimes also thought of as a kind of "chemistry" between them. Indeed, it would be hard to find a word more ambiguous.

Married love, however, which is relatively rare, even among couples who have, in the customary sense, been long married with no thought of divorce, is unique in its depth and permanence. Once established, it does indeed last until its partners are separated by death. And, it is important to note, it can exist even between lifetime partners who are not legally married at all; for example, homosexual partners, or a man and a woman who never bothered to legalize their relationship but nevertheless live as man and wife. These are the truly married, whatever the law might say.

Unless such distinctions are clearly understood it will be impossible to understand the idea of married love that is here presented. And it must be especially noted that we are *not* saying that people who "get married," in the conventional sense, and manage to stay married, are automatically bound together by married love. More often, they are not.

Now this kind of love, we have also said, rests upon, and in fact is one and the same, as the *mutual fulfillment of needs*. And this, too, needs explaining.

We are not here referring to what are thought of as basic needs, such as the need for economic security, sexual compatibility, and safety from violence and abuse, important as these are. Instead, we are referring to that vast array of needs that arise from the self-love that governs everything we do. These are for the most part what everyone would rightly regard as trivial, and yet, their being met is absolutely basic to individual happiness and, especially, the deep happiness that is sometimes found in marriage.

When married partners drift apart, both becoming more and more absorbed in their own needs and increasingly unaware of the other's, then the marriage slowly dies. Here, for example, is an all too common marital history, even in marriages which, unlike this one, do not end in divorce:

It wasn't until we actually separated that I realized how far we had, over time, drifted apart. I realized that I did not even know where, in this small city, my wife worked, nor did I have any clear idea what she did. I was too absorbed in myself to wonder. And she was the same with me. My work took me from city to city, and while she knew more or less where I was at any given time, she didn't know what I was doing there, because she never asked. She, too, had her mind on her own things, and had simply lost track of me. This mutual lack of awareness and concern went on for several years, increasing all the time, without either of us realizing what was happening. Outwardly our life together continued as usual, with dinner in some nice restaurant about once a week, and all the usual keeping of company. But we had, finally, become strangers to each other, and didn't know it until it was over.

What we have before us now are three basic ideas, namely, *married love*, *the fulfillment of needs*, and the *sense of self-worth*. They are all related to each other. Indeed, married love we have defined as the mutual fulfillment of needs. It is on this, and this alone, that genuine marriage rests. It is not anything that is rare, and the understanding of it is not difficult, but it is also not common. If it were the common possession of all married couples, then there would be no such thing as divorce.

What we are referring to, then, can be described simply as *paying attention to*. This has already been touched upon in our discussion of the sense of self-worth.

For example, a woman, however modest, who is at all attractive, is sensitive to this, and while her husband's disregard of this will not destroy the marriage, it will nevertheless dampen the love upon which marriage must rest. It should never be disregarded. For example, he should *notice* what she is wearing from one day to another, and when it is something especially appealing, not fail to comment. He should notice whenever she has her hair done, or has prepared a meal that is especially good, or when she expresses herself singularly well. A woman is likely to have unique talents, like a talent for poetic expression, or perhaps she paints well, or is an especially good gardener—anything of this sort has a direct connection with her sense of self-worth. Things like this may be trivial in themselves, but her sense of self-worth is not. It is what gives her life meaning from moment to moment. Constant awareness of these things convey the single, all-important message: *You count, you are important.* A marriage that nourishes this sense of self-worth, even in the smallest sense, lasts, provided it is reciprocated. One that does not will not necessarily end in divorce, but it will not flourish, either.

All this would seem hardly worth dwelling on were it not so sorely lacking in so many marriages. Where it is lacking, the partners, though they may not feel utterly unloved, nevertheless feel taken for granted.

Of course it should go without saying that this works both ways. Husbands, too, can feel taken for granted. We all have our little strengths and virtues that we delight in, even though we make no big thing of them. For example, a man may take pride in his golf stroke even though it does not measure up to that of a master, or perhaps of his grace when he dances, or his aplomb when he addresses an audience, or what he imagines to be his subtle wit, and so on. *Notice these.* Even if there is some small virtue that you have commented on a thousand times, notice it again the next time it is displayed. These are just some of the dozens of different ways that one says: You are an unusual human being. It is a message that no one ever tires of hearing. All of us prize what we have, what it is that, we imagine, sets us apart from everyone else. Truly great human beings are of course rare, but everyone wants to think of himself or herself as somehow special. There can be nothing wrong with this. If there were, then it would not be so universal.

Here there must be no misunderstanding. We are not urging flattery or manipulation. Praises must be honest and genuine. The flatterer is someone who pretends admiration which is not felt, in order to ingratiate himself or to manipulate the other. It is a form of basic dishonesty. Moreover, it is almost impossible to conceal. If someone compliments you on something you know you lack, then you see through this, if not immediately, then sooner or later. It cannot succeed. You know when you are being flattered, which is of course not the worst of wrongs, but when used to manipulate, it is a serious wrong. Loving a person is loving her for what she is, not for what she can do for you. You love her beauty because she possesses it, even if only to a modest degree. Since it means something to her, it means something to you, too. And so with every other virtue, small or great. Even though she may excel at something for which you have no talent at all, such as, for example, poetry, you do genuinely love her achievements there whether anyone else does or not. To merely pretend this is to flatter and ingratiate; it is to be thinking of yourself, rather than of her.

Most of my examples have had to do with a man's treatment of his wife, rather than the other way around, and in fact, it is men who, as a rule, tend to fall short here. Women can be insensitive to their husbands, to be sure, but they are less likely to be. Of the dozens of divorced people I have interviewed, the most common reason women gave for failure in their marriages was, as we have noted, "he was boring." Sometimes other causes were cited—adultery, dishonesty, that sort of thing—but far outnumbering these grave faults was the common one, that he failed to notice them, took them for granted. Once a man has over the entire period of courtship used every device to ingratiate himself, scrupulously noting his partner's every good point, then once he *has* her, he is likely to think that there is no longer any point to this. There is no better way to express this than to say that he takes her for granted. She becomes a possession that needs no further polishing. He becomes a bore. And the scene is set for a quick dissolution of the marriage in case some other person fills the vacuum he has created. He will declare that she was faithless, but in truth, she was more driven from the marriage than lured.

What is being referred to here, as the fulfillment of needs, often fails in more clear-cut ways than simple neglect. One of the most common, for example, is the subtle "put-down." Here a partner is not simply ignored, but rather, singled out for a defeat which is made to appear as something else. The spouse does not merely fail to note favorably some small virtue, but turns it upside down. For example, suppose her husband has taken up playing the harmonica and is making some progress, though he has a long way to go. His wife comments, with feigned humor that disguises the sarcasm, that he can already play "My Country Tis of Thee." The comment is of course *true*, he can indeed do that, but it is not said in praise. It admits no rebuttal, and the sting is slight, but nonetheless real.

Or consider the following trivial example that came up in one of my interviews:

> I was serving as chairperson of the committee that served the eld-erly in various ways, and after one such meeting I felt good for having managed it all especially well. Two people actually com-mented on this. When I got home and mentioned it to my husband, his reaction was: "Ah! We all need our little triumphs, don't we?"

Of course, it *was* a small achievement, but an achievement just the same. And, of course, what he said was incontestably true. But it was a put-down. And what is especially significant here is that she still remembered it, with a sense of hurt, years later, long after her husband had died. He perhaps thought the sarcasm was an expression of wit. Instead, it was an attempt to enhance his sense of worth by reducing hers.

It would be a simple matter, but tiresome, to multiply such examples. We have all seen them, in the couple that is given to quibbling or low-key bickering, in husbands or wives who effu-sively praise something in another person that is manifestly lacking in their spouses, that is an oblique put-down. For example, a hus-band, in the presence of his overweight wife, comments on the lovely figure of some passerby. What makes this kind of slight so effective, and ultimately destructive, is that there is no possible response, except, perhaps, a subtle dig in the other's direction. The one who has been slighted is alert for the chance to pay back.

These are all examples of slight wounds, but the point is that they are wounds, and no marriage was ever made good by repeatedly inflicting them. They go a step beyond mere taking for granted, the way, for example, we take for granted some stranger. But they are steps in the wrong direction, and the damage is cumulative. Perhaps nothing is more effective in reducing a marriage to humdrum than this sort of thing. Couples who never quarrel, never raise their voices at each other, and whose marriages do not actually come to pieces, nevertheless reduce them to lifelong mediocrity by just this kind of inconsiderateness.

The needs that one brings to a marriage form a kind of hierarchy, those of the kind just considered being at the bottom. At the top would be such things as the need for security and safety, which can be violated by extreme poverty or spousal abuse, or freedom to make one's own day-to-day choices and decisions, which is violated by a controlling husband. It is not surprising that when these needs are unfulfilled, love dies, even when the outward form of marriage is preserved. Many women have endured controlling husbands, or even abusive ones, and many men have endured critical and nagging wives, but nothing resembling genuine love can thrive in such conditions.

In between the trivial, day-to-day needs, which are often idiosyncratic, and the very basic ones shared by all, there is a whole continuum. Here should be placed such things as the need for cooperation, affection, intimacy, and so on—all of the needs that we normally associate with deep love.

Yet, the point must be reiterated, that it is the trivial needs, the little wants and preferences that are *not* shared by all, that matter overwhelmingly, simply because they are so varied and numerous and often unnoticed and thus unmet. They make the difference between marriages that flourish and are a great blessing to their partners, and those that just limp along.

Finally, it should be noted that nothing has been said here concerning sex and the needs that this creates. It has not been mentioned, because it is so obvious. But more important, those needs are *not* the basis for the enduring love that we have been describing. Some persons may of course derive some of their sense of self-worth from sexual capacities or prowess, but this is assuredly not why sexual intimacy is important to marriage. The point of such intimacy is not to show off, or, if it is, then something is clearly out of balance.

What we have been talking about are, once again, the small needs that everyone has from one moment to the next. When these are met, constantly and with sincere appreciation, marriage thrives, even sometimes when the more basic needs are not met. This is the kind of love that is sustained "for richer, for poorer, in sickness and in health," which surely means that these are the ones that matter, more than economic security, more even than health. Love is not just the keeping of vows. Unless supported by the sense of self-worth, which sickness or poverty can seldom extinguish, marriage vows are little more than poetry, nice for embellishing a wedding, but hardly more lasting than that.

Does all this mean that we should regard our spouses as being without fault? That one should never criticize? Certainly not. What it does mean is that faults should never be seized upon in a way that can erode the sense of self-worth. There is nothing wrong with correcting someone you care about if the correction is in fact well meant, and will be taken as such. Common faults, such as extravagance or untidiness, can often be constructively commented on, without the other person feeling put down. This is simply a matter of tact. There are, on the other hand, incorrigible faults, that is, things that simply cannot be changed, and these must be utterly ignored. Consider, for example, a woman who is given to giggling, and has done so all her life. If she knows it annoys, then she can try to control it perhaps, but for her husband to constantly express annoyance does nothing for her at all. Or consider a husband who simply cannot be trained to pick things up. Leaving things scattered about is just his way of doing things, and always has been. Again, nothing is gained by constantly expressing annoyance at this.

Of course there are faults that are incorrigible and serious, and these are a different matter altogether. Often, in the face of these, the only solution is divorce. Some men, for example, are abusive, if not by nature then by lifelong practice, and are likely to be beyond hope. Or a woman might be given to perpetual nagging, and apparently incapable of changing this. Or, even more seriously, she may be incorrigibly hostile to stepchildren, devastating to her husband's pride in them, thus rendering the family life all but impossible. Things like this are not among the day-to-day needs and frustrations that have been the subject of our discussion.

There is, of course, no one simple key to married love and marital happiness. There are great differences between people and between the relationships they form. So we are not saying here that if partners simply cultivate an awareness of each other, and take care to meet the simple ordinary needs upon which the sense of self-worth rests, then happiness will surely follow. What we *have* done is call attention to, and dwell upon, a basic fact of human nature that underlies every marriage that is genuinely and lastingly happy, and the reason this has been singled out is that, notwithstanding its universality, it is almost never well understood. And neglect of it is the cause of more unhappiness in marriage than anything else—more important than the obvious things, like infidelity, abuse, and outright neglect.

A marriage whose partners are constantly aware of each other, and not just absorbed in themselves, is not just one that lasts. It is a marriage that confers on both, not just love, but the constant joy of being in love. This is easily destroyed, usually by simple neglect, but it is also easily nourished. You need only to step out of yourself, and to see, totally, the person you so confidently expected to love forever.

DIVORCE AND FRIENDSHIP

The tendency to think in terms of absolutes applies especially to the concept of marriage. For example, we think that a person is either married or single. It is hard to think of marriage as something that admits of degrees. Instead, we speak of good marriages and bad marriages.

But that is not realistic. For example, a man and a woman who have shared their love and their lives totally for years, living as a married couple in every respect except for there being no documentation in a hall of records, are surely more married than a couple who never got around to getting divorce but have been separated and totally out of touch with each other for decades.

Our thinking of divorce involves stereotypes of the same kind. Thus, we think of a divorced pair as, at best, strangers to each other and, more commonly, as enemies, often bitter ones. The divorced spouse is often not invited to social gatherings where his or her former spouse is likely to be present because of the discomfort this would create all around. Friends of a divorced woman are not expected to retain friendship with her ex-husband, and vice versa.

But divorce need not be like that and, for some particularly high-minded and intelligent people, it sometimes is not. Here are three examples:

> I was one of a large number of junior faculty of a university and we socialized regularly. Over time we came to know each other well, and considerable flirting went on. Eventually I came to feel that I had more in common with the wife of one of my best friends than with my own wife, and oddly enough, her husband came to feel about the same with respect to my wife. There was nothing really improper in this, and we all were quite aware of the strong friendships that were developing. In time I found myself quite in love with my friend's wife, and amazingly, he with mine. After a lot of talk and thinking, and considerable agonizing, my wife and I separated, and, soon after, so did the other

couple, and we all gravitated to what seemed to be our true loves. We in effect swapped partners and got remarried. What is most interesting about this strange development, however, is that our larger social life went on exactly as before, except that the flirting stopped, at least between us four, no jealousy erupted, and everyone remained friends, even more than before.

After years of what seemed to us both to be a perfect marriage my wife found herself in love with another woman. She had not hitherto suspected that sexual orientation. This did, however, spell the absolute destruction of our marriage. There simply was no way we could go on like that. I was utterly devastated and, at first, profoundly resentful. I imagined all sorts of ways to make it hard, maybe impossible, for her to leave me, and my anger toward that other woman, who had quite openly undertaken to destroy my marriage, was enormous. I eventually realized that trying to sustain a marriage under these circumstances could, at best, result only in a living hell, and, more important, I realized that any lashing out on my part, and attempt to assuage my resentment through hurtful acts, would only result in misery for me as well as her, to say nothing about the damage to our young children.

What I resolved to do, then, was cultivate as good a friendship as I could with my wife, even after she had abandoned me, and, even more important, to somehow establish a kind of friendship with that other woman. This latter was made less difficult by her apparently feeling some guilt over the whole matter, and welcoming any friendly gesture I could put forth.

The friendship I established with my faithless wife, workable even if never close, paid off. She had no resources whatever, and I helped her there, buying her a house and paying all the expenses of her professional training. This cost me dearly, but it was worth it. She never reached for any weapon against me, has never spoken a word against me, and things have remained civil, even if not warm. Our children remained undamaged, and we have never engaged in any conflict over them.

It was not hard to build a kind of friendship with the other woman. She reciprocated every friendly gesture I made, neither of us trying to get one up on the other. She bakes me a beautiful pie for my birthday every year, and we both cultivate an affability at every encounter. I even arranged to have her made the legal guardian of the children in the unlikely event both my ex-wife and I should die, and this brought tears to her eyes.

I never got to take out my deep resentment and disappointment. I had robbed myself of that opportunity. I do not know whether they appreciate that or not, but what I do know is that no weapons were drawn against me, either, and it was more than worth it.

My wife and I had been married for over twenty years. It was a good, stable marriage, but during the last four years we had been drifting apart without either of us being quite aware of it. She was a social worker, and I realized one day that I didn't even know where she worked, or quite what the nature of her work was. I realized, too, that she had about as little awareness of or interest in what I was doing from one day to another. We had, through no overt acts, become strangers. I eventually found myself drawn to another woman, leading to a shameful affair, eventually discovered by my wife. She, without second thought, wanted out of the marriage. I could hardly object, and, indeed, by that time I had no desire to object.

This sordid turn of events did not, fortunately, produce enmity on her part. On the contrary, she seemed happy now to lead her own life, totally independent of me. In fact it was better than this, for we became true friends, better than we had been before. We had fairly frequent lunches and dinners together, each of us was always welcome in the other's house, bitter words were never spoken, and when I remarried and became a father again it was she who suggested the name that my son now has. I wept when she died, partly from guilt, but also from sorrow, for the friendship that had been created by divorce rather than by what had been created by marriage.

It is, then, possible for divorced people to remain friends and even to build a degree of affection on a divorce. This is, of course, rare. Most divorced people revert to childishness, trading blows, sometimes for years, and always at great cost to themselves, both emotionally and in measurable expense.

Is it possible to actually *enhance* marriage by divorce? This seems like a contradiction. How can divorced people be in any sense still married, much less have a loving marriage? It is possible, though of course very rare, and it is inspiring. Consider this true account.

> After we were divorced my ex-husband developed pancreatic cancer, from which he had no chance whatever of recovering. He was lonely and miserable, and could look forward only to steady and eventually deeply painful decline. I moved back with him and, for the year that remained of his life, I became his totally caring and loving partner. In a superficial way it was a lost year for me, but in every way that counts, it was the most rewarding year of my life. I was saddened beyond measure when death finally claimed him, and I have certainly never regretted what I did.

It is misleading to describe this as a marriage built upon a divorce. It was built upon compassion. Still, during that year these two were, in every way that counts, more truly married than they had been before and, indeed, more than most people ever are.

While friendship can sometimes be enhanced by divorce, can a loving marriage actually be *improved* by or even rest upon divorce? This, again, seems like a contradiction—to be more totally married through divorce than before—but it has happened. No generalization can be drawn from this. It would be absurd to say that divorce is an appropriate pathway to true marriage, but there is at least one circumstance in which this can actually happen. It will be described here, not as a curiosity, but as shedding light on what true marriage is.

Medicaid (not to be confused with Medicare) is a program administered in every state to help the indigent deal with costly illness. The idea behind it is obviously good; the poor should not be denied care just because they cannot afford it. Poverty is defined in terms of total assets, that is, income, plus such assets as real estate, intangible property, and so on.

The rule is that, in the case of married people, such income and assets amount to the total possessed by both partners. Thus, if one partner becomes seriously ill with ongoing disease, requiring costly care, then that partner is not eligible for Medicaid until the assets of both partners taken together fall below a certain line, the assumption being that married people have a responsibility to take care of each other.

Consider, then, a late-life marriage—say, a woman who, in her fifties, marries. Suppose further that she has assets, her lifetime savings, of, let us suppose, fifty thousand dollars. A year or two later her husband contracts a dreaded disease, one that will be costly, and finally, terminal. It will consume all of his resources to pay for this care and, after he has been reduced to poverty, the gargantuan bills will have to be paid by his wife until, finally, they together fall below the poverty line. He has lost everything, and so has she, but now Medicaid will take over for the costs that remain.

One way to avoid that dreadful situation would be for them to divorce, thereby protecting her assets. Should they do it? Will it not appear that she is abandoning her husband just when he needs her most?

Of course not. The technicality of divorce need have no bearing whatsoever on their relationship. Their marriage can continue exactly as before—totally loving and committed. She in no sense abandons him. The two have simply taken advantage of the provisions of law to guard her lifetime savings, which would never have been threatened had she not married. No one has misrepresented anything.

On the positive side, it can be seen that such a step can only enhance the marriage. The marriage is made better by the divorce. The wife is not put in the position of seeing her life savings drained to nothing and, at the same time, the enormous expenses thrust upon them are painlessly met. Love, instead of resentment and depression, grows. The husband retains his wife's love, and she need never be tempted to think that, perhaps, it would have been better not to marry at all.

Some might say that a wife who took advantage of the law in this way would simply be shoving her responsibilities off onto government, that is, taxpayers, but that, whether correct or not, is not what is at issue here. The story simply illustrates, once again, the main theme of this book; namely, that people are not made married by any conventional ceremony and the filing of documents, as is so widely assumed, but by the mutual fulfillment of needs.

I have no direct experience of this happening, but I am told by attorneys that it does happen. It is an obvious solution to what could otherwise be a very destructive situation.

Stereotypes are hard to overcome, however. People do think of marriage as arising from a wedding and the filing of documents. This was driven home to me by the following true story:

My wife's sense of security was excessively bound up with ownership. She had considerable assets, accumulated through inheritance before we married, while mine were meager in comparison. She was constantly tempted to buy useless real estate, simply with the aim of owning it. At one point she explored the possibility of buying a woodland, for which she would have no use whatsoever, just so she could, as she expressed it, "go sit in the middle of it." Even my life insurance, under which she was already the sole beneficiary, was pointlessly transferred to her ownership.

It was not surprising, then, that it would occur to her that extended illness on my part might jeopardize her assets. Mine could be eaten up, and then hers would be invaded. So she raised the question whether we should become divorced, but with the understanding that this would change nothing in our relationship, which neither of us had any intention of altering. We were thoroughly married and expected to preserve our love and fidelity forever.

So I asked an attorney whether he thought this would be a

prudent step. His response: "Well, if I were the judge, I would just treat you like the rat that abandons the sinking ship." Divorce, to him, as with virtually everyone else, meant the destruction of a relationship. He was unable to think of it as based upon mutual fulfillment, which is my definition of marital love. Yet, if you think through the situation I have described, even though it is not common, then you get a far more realistic conception of true marriage.

BEING IN LOVE

If you want to know what it's like to be in love, don't look enviously at newlyweds, don't read romance novels, listen to popular music, or watch films or television. Look, instead, at some elderly couple, long married, he in a baggy suit, she in a shapeless dress, not rich and not poor, perhaps out walking, and yes, perhaps holding hands. They know each other's likes and dislikes, and they talk, pretty much, about the things they've always talked about. For them it truly is "'til death do us part," and they need no promises to insure that. It rests on the years of knowing, needing, and loving each other.

You can see this sometimes in a couple long married, with loving children and perhaps grandchildren. They do not swoon with joy, but neither do they bicker or put each other down with subtle comments that are unflattering. They take each other for granted, in the sense that it would not occur to either to doubt the fidelity and constancy of the other. They know each other totally, almost to the point of reading each other's thoughts and emotions from one hour to the next. Age and hard work may have left their marks, but these have not dimmed their contentment, especially when they are together. These people, though they may be old, without wealth, and pretty much unknown to the world, are in love. And they are happy.

An elderly man, probably in his eighties, described his feelings this way:

When I'm in the house alone, I'm all right, but I don't function very efficiently. I just sort of mark time. Little things I should be doing get put off, and I look at the clock from time to time, waiting for her to come back. I always know approximately when she'll get home, and when she does, I feel alive again, just having her there. If she's up in her room, working at her things, I feel okay, because I know she's there, but then, when she comes back down, for lunch or to fix dinner or whatever, I totally come to life, even though nothing else happens, nothing dramatic. It's always like this, day after day, year after year, and there was a time, long ago, when it would surprise me, this sudden change of mood and feeling. I know my life would be completely empty without her. I get a taste of this once in a great while, when something keeps her away from home overnight. I feel empty, I can't sleep, and sometimes I've thought to myself, What if I didn't have her? It is the unthinkable thought. I would simply be dead.

That, in its simple banality, is a genuine love story.

Or is it, on the contrary, a mark of unnatural dependence? Not if it is not exploited. Someone with a highly dependent personality is vulnerable to control, but that was not the case here. This old man conveyed the unmistakable impression of fulfillment, the result of decades of selfless affections, and his wife, whom I met, appeared to be the embodiment of sweetness.

How did they get there? Not by power, riches, or fame, for they have none of these. And not by the marriage having been launched by a great and flamboyant wedding, for the euphoria that accompanies this is perhaps the most short-lived happiness there is. And not by their marriage vows, so solemnly uttered, for these guarantee nothing. All marriages begin with vows of everlasting love, but they have no lasting force.

Love that is lasting rests on one thing only, something that is easy to state but not easy to understand, and that is the mutual fulfillment of needs.

Sex and Marriage

It is very doubtful whether a single marriage has ever been sustained solely by the sexual fulfillment of its partners, even though this impulse is often the main ingredient of falling in love. It is always the lesser, moment-to-moment needs that count, and it is these upon which married love rests even when, due to sickness, age, or whatever, sexual activity becomes minimal to nonexistent.

Until the 1950s female sexuality was almost universally misunderstood. The shock came with Alfred Kinsey's publication of his vast research on the subject. His studies of male sexuality evoked little surprise, beyond the fact that it had become the subject of serious research, but it was far otherwise with respect to women. It was until then widely assumed that sex played only a minimal role in female psychology. Women were thought of as submitting, perhaps happily, but without passion. The discovery—and it was hardly less than this—that women lust after their husbands just as their husbands do after them, that they lust for perfect strangers as well, and that they are given to lurid sexual fantasy, just as men and boys are, came as a great shock. It was something that simply had not been talked about, and was assumed to have little significance. The reason, of course, was not that this did not exist, but that custom forbade associating it with the fair sex. Even the pope, years later, in his pronouncements on marriage, seemed ignorant of it.

To some extent we still think in those terms, notwithstanding our intellectual understanding of the realities. We still think of sexual activity as initiated by a man, something he does, his partner being the recipient. This is not without any basis in male psychology. Men and women, quite apart from the strength of this impulse as it operates in both, do think of sex differently. A man tends to assume that his role is to *perform*, and he takes pride in his sexual prowess, attaching great importance to his ability to sustain a strong erection, to impress, to be pleased with himself. Women rarely think this way. They are more likely to want to feel desired.

Hence the enormous popularity among men of drugs that promote sexual vigor, and the more common concern among women for youth and beauty, the appeal of their physical shape, and so on. These are commonplace observations, which, like all generalizations, of course admit of exceptions.

What still needs to be stressed, however, is that sex in marriage is not just an occasional or frequent indulgence, but must be treated in the same way as all other needs: with constant awareness of the feelings of one's partner. Self-indulgence is as out of place here as it is in every other aspect of marriage. The secret of married love is constant awareness, something that is easy to forget in the throes of passion. No woman wants to be used as a mere instrument of her husband's lust, no matter how impressed he may be with himself, and no man needs a wife who is little more that the passive recipient of his act. There are wives who, from failure on their husbands' part, never experience joy in sex at all, and men who, from failure on their wives' part, are drawn instead to other women, found to be exciting. Sometimes a woman wants more than to be held, and sometimes a man wishes to reverse the roles and be the passive partner to his wife's outrageous advances. In any case, what matters is not so much the act, as the ongoing awareness of needs, which can change from moment to moment.

chapter 3
failed marriages

WHY MARRIAGES FAIL

Typically, divorcing people or those contemplating divorce assign the blame to the other partner—"He wouldn't let me do anything," "She just wanted to spend everything we had," and so on. Sometimes the complaint takes the form of something very specific and irreparable, like "She had this thyroid problem that made life sometimes unbearable for everyone," or "He had an uncontrollable temper and his anger would burst forth unpredictably over nothing."

Often there is truth in such complaints, but more often they serve to conceal the truth rather than to explain anything. Indeed, the motive is often, perhaps usually, only the need to deflect blame from oneself. It has to be the other person's *fault*. The underlying message is that, except for the fault, we could have had a perfectly good marriage; certainly *I* did everything right. Self-vindication is the driving motive. Sometimes a divorced person will say, naively, "I don't know why she/he left," from that same motive.

Sometimes, to be sure, a marriage does fail because of some real or incorrigible fault—alcoholism or drug addiction, for example, or ongoing physical abuse, or indiscriminate womanizing, or actual physical abandonment, or imprisonment, things that are quite specific, apparent to anyone, and intolerable.

Usually, however, the explanations are not like this. Often they have to do with alleged character defects, like being too "self-centered," or "selfish," or "insensitive," "immature," and so on. And indeed, sometimes they amount to sheer abstractions, like "we were not compatible," or "she lacked self-esteem," or "his father set impossible goals for him as a kid." Real understanding becomes impossible as soon as you start down roads like this. You fool yourself into thinking you have explained something.

Sometimes a marriage fails because of some surprise occurrence—the discovery of a love affair, for example—but usually it is slow and undetected by its partners. Decay is not a momentary event, but a slow process, usually with no apparent signs, no red flags. And then, one day, one or both partners wake up to the realization that they are deeply unhappy with each other. Disintegration is then swift and irreversible.

Here, for example, is a brief account of what, except for the details, happens over and over:

We were married for seventeen years and had a daughter, now grown up. We seldom quarreled, there were almost never any expressions of anger other than the mild irritations that are a part of normal life. It seemed like a good, stable marriage. We had a social life, dined out together fairly often, went to the theater, and to hear good music, all the normal things that well-educated married people do. But then, I realized I was not very happy, and could see my husband wasn't, either. I began to realize that things had not been all that good for a long time. He is an engineer, something for which I have no understanding, and my interests are literary, and quite foreign to him, but of course, that had been true from the start. We never thought it mattered. But finally I realized that we were living in separate worlds, emotionally and intellectually. He had his study and I had mine, and there was less and less interaction between us as time went along. We did the things we had always done, but it was from habit, not from any need to be together. It got to the point that, while we never fought about anything, we also never talked with each other, beyond the usual more or less meaningless and banal conversation. At the end he seemed to have withdrawn completely, and I suppose I had, too, and that is when I learned that for months he had been involved with another woman. The marriage was over. It didn't end with a bang, there were no sudden dramatic developments, not even any recriminations, just a slow death.

Why did that marriage fail? Not because something suddenly went wrong, not because either partner had some deep and intolerable fault, and not because of adultery, although anyone satisfied with superficial explanations would certainly point to this as the cause. It is to the credit of the person who supplied this account that she did not.

What happened is terribly simple, and it is what almost always happens in marriages that come apart. The partners simply were not meeting each other's needs. At first it worked, because needs were being met—they had a child to raise, much loved by both, and they had long-range goals they needed to reach cooperatively—specifically, to attain financial security. But the daughter grew up, and there came a day when material security was no longer threatened. All they had was each other, and they no longer needed each other.

Here is another account, significant because, until it finally came apart, the marriage seemed to possess every mark of stability. Its partners were strong believers in what are known as family values, were never known to quarrel, and seemed the very epitome of a happily married couple:

We've been married for over thirty years, and for most of that time our marriage was the model of strength and stability. My wife took home and family very seriously indeed, and so did I. My professional career soared beyond what anyone could have expected, and we seemed in every respect to have it made—a good, prosperous life, cottage on the seashore, and beautiful children. My wife's interest in church reinforced our family values, and I was happy to go along with it.

Things began to change after our kids left home for college. We no longer focused on them, but on each other. Her interest in religion intensified, and she was ordained in a main-line Protestant church. She became the minister of a small church nearby, and I helped her in many ways with respect to planning and administration of church affairs.

A few years later my work took me to London for a couple years. My wife went with me, of course, but quickly came to dislike everything about it—the weather, transportation, and the people with whom she seemed to have very little in common. Worst of all, she could not find any church to work with, and so, after only a brief trial, she left for home. There she was able to establish herself in a new church, a small one in a little town in Kansas, and this became the center of her life.

She became increasingly spiritual, and I came more and more to feel left out. I left England and found new and exciting work in San Francisco, where I hoped she would join me, since it seemed to me there were abundant opportunities for church work there, but she chose instead to stay in Kansas, which offered no opportunities at all for me. It seemed to me that her little church had become more important to her than her marriage. On top of this her absorption in things spiritual intensified. She read devotional literature, which meant little to me, and if we were in some interesting city, she just wanted to visit churches, to the exclusion of what seemed to me to be far more interesting things to see. I like hiking and the out-of-doors generally, but she wanted, instead, to do what was called "labyrinth" exercises. These consist of slowly working one's way to the center of a maze-like arrangement, seeking spiritual improvement, and hopefully finding a kind of enlightenment at the center. All this left me cold.

I don't know what's in store for us now. She wants me to give up my challenging work in San Francisco and move to Kansas, where I would perish of boredom. And she refuses to consider moving to San Francisco. We have simply gone our separate ways, and I see no way to restore the marriage we once had.

In this account we see, once again, the role of need fulfillment in binding a couple together. They needed each other for parenting, but when their children were grown, other needs took over and each found fulfillment in ways that did not involve the other. As their mutual fulfillment of needs declined, so did their love, these two things being, in fact, one and the same.

SUDDEN SUCCESS

Marital failure is often, paradoxically, precipitated, though not caused, by the sudden success of one of its partners. A struggling writer, for example, suddenly finds acceptance: his first novel is acclaimed by reviewers, or his stories begin appearing in a prestigious literary magazine, or he wins a poetry prize—that sort of thing. And of course it can happen on the other side: a wife, whose life has been humdrum, wins a coveted award for outstanding teaching, or becomes the first woman to gain partnership in a law firm, or whatever. Here the effect is not unlike that of an illicit affair, wherein a wife finds herself appreciated for her special talents, to a degree that was always lacking in her marriage. Marriage partners always have a tendency to take each other for granted. When something from outside the marriage lifts one out of this status, whether it be worldly recognition or a lover's attention, the result is rapid erosion of the marriage, often its complete destruction. It is simply, once again, a matter of needs being fulfilled that are not being met in the marriage. *Everyone* has a deep need for recognition, for success, which sometimes comes with great suddenness. It can be something dramatic, such as receipt of a widely coveted award, or something much less so, like a great increase in salary or professional status. What is significant in something like this is not so much that one is suddenly richer, but that one is suddenly vindicated in the sense of self-worth.

Here, for example, is something quite common in a failed marriage:

> My wife and I had what appeared to be a perfectly stable marriage. There was no significant quarreling, our middle-class backgrounds were similar, our income, though modest, was adequate, we enjoyed doing things together, and we had an active social life. We also had two beautiful young children, and the obvious happiness and outgoing nature of these children was a good measure of the happiness and stability of our home life. Given all this, our friends were astounded when, after about ten years, the marriage quite suddenly began to come apart.
>
> That was a long time ago, and when I look back now it isn't hard to see what happened. My wife struggled with me through the hungry years of graduate school, and then I got a lower-level appointment to a good, liberal arts college. That went well, and I was liked by my students and by the faculty. I settled comfortably in the academic life, lunching at the faculty club, joining into the stimulating social life of my colleagues, and my wife and I were both happy in the normal life we had and its simple day-to-day activities. We neither expected nor sought anything more.
>
> My work then took on new meaning when, suddenly, one of my poems was accepted by a literary journal, and then, soon after, more of the same. Before long a small book of my poems came out and was acclaimed by significant critics. All this began to go to my head, and I began to feel like something more than just another college teacher. Soon I was receiving invitations from major universities to give readings, as well as offers for tenured professorships. I got an award for study in England, and this was followed by promotion to a named professorship in an Ivy League university.

Now I can identify in my mind the very hour, almost, that I realized my marriage was over. It was at a party, on the evening that I had been notified of a very large salary increase. I didn't then connect all this with the disintegration of my marriage, but I did, that evening, somehow realize that the marriage no longer had much meaning for me. I knew that I was deeply unhappy, deeply dissatisfied with my home life, and I vaguely wanted out. My wife seemed completely out of tune with my thoughts and feelings, even though she had not changed at all in all those years, and no bitter words had been exchanged. The marriage had lost its importance for me, but the realization of this had been slow in coming.

Was it a mistake? Maybe, if you look at it superficially. After all, one would think that worldly success, which everyone seeks, would strengthen home life. But on the other hand, what can you do with deep, intractable unhappiness, except try to escape from it?

If there is a moral to be gleaned from this, it is that worldly success can come at a high price for marriage. Sudden celebrity is so often destructive of marriage that is comes as a surprise sometimes to learn of a marriage that survives it. Couples often struggle through near poverty on the way to a medical degree only to find their marriage soon in ruins as a result of the new and prosperous life that such a degree makes possible. An enormously successful businessman is easy prey for a glamorous outsider. To say that worldly success and stable marriage cannot go together would be absurd, of course, but they very often do not.

INFIDELITY

Adultery is, by itself, in every jurisdiction a sufficient ground for divorce, and in some jurisdictions it was once the only one recognized under law. This led to enormously destructive policies. For example, a petitioner's lawyer arranges for photographers to sneak up on an adulterous couple, perhaps in a motel, and catch their behavior on film, which will then be submitted in court as proof. It would be impossible to imagine anything more destructive in creating lifelong enmity between a divorcing couple. It is the ultimate invasion of privacy, the final humiliation, a total assault upon a person's sense of self-worth.

Treating infidelity as being, by itself, a sufficient ground for divorce is a reflection of the age-old concept of marriage as a contractual arrangement. Two people, it is imagined, have by their vows contracted to enter into a relationship, each, presumably, with the view to advancing his or her self-interest, however that may be conceived. Each has pledged to "forsake all others," and the one who has failed has broken the contract.

This, then, is what infidelity has come to mean—sexual misconduct. What it really means, however, is breach of faith or trust, and there are many ways in which this can occur that have nothing to do with sex.

For example, a husband or wife who maintains a secret bank account, or who refuses to disclose to the other his or her financial resources, violates a trust. Indeed, *any* deception amounts to infidelity. A man who keeps secret company with other women is, indeed, unfaithful, but so is one who keeps secret company with other men, perhaps for unlawful purposes. If marriage rests at all on fidelity, as it surely does, then any marital alliance that falls short of total trust and honesty also falls short of true marriage.

The reduction, then, of the concept of marital fidelity to mere sexual exclusiveness is another example of stereotypical or simplistic thinking, and it can lead to strange inferences. For example, most persons would be unlikely to find anything strange in saying of a wife, who had long since lost all love for her husband, that she nevertheless remained faithful to him to the end. If marriage is a relationship bound by lasting love, then to withdraw that love is to commit the ultimate infidelity, whether any third person is involved or not.

Perhaps the true nature of infidelity can be seen by concocting an example. Imagine a man who has been long married to one person and who has never lapsed from the rule of strict sexual constancy, and would never be suspected of this either by his wife or by anyone who knows him. He is, at least in this respect, a model of rectitude. But now suppose that this same man, perhaps from inhibitions nourished by religion, or other factors in his upbringing, has an aversion to sex. He has never yielded to temptation, because he has never been tempted. His intimacy with his wife is perfunctory, infrequent, and quite devoid of joy for either of them. They are, in fact, strangers to each other's deeper feelings. In the light of this, does not his fidelity to his wife become something less impressive?

Now add to this that this husband is driven by greed and penuriousness and keeps secret from his wife what his resources are. We can suppose that he has several undisclosed bank accounts, into which, over time, he squirrels away a considerable fortune, his wife all the while believing that he is hard-working and poor, so that she feels compelled to augment their income through an otherwise unrewarding and meaningless job. Has the rule of fidelity been breached?

Further, suppose that the wife of this dreary marriage is stricken with incurable cancer, resulting in prolonged and eventually painful decline. At this point her husband loses any interest he ever had in her and looks forward to her demise. Still, of course, he has no inclination to sexual misconduct of any kind. Can he still be described as a faithful husband?

And finally, imagine that this wife has been drawn into a love affair with another man, who genuinely cares for her, without reserve, even through her long illness. Has she broken faith? Has she a husband in any meaningful sense to be unfaithful to?

Clearly, she has been married in name only, and unfaithful only in the narrowest sense, which has little meaning here. It is her "husband" who has been faithless. Yet many, perhaps most persons, victimized by the stereotypical and legalistic notion of fidelity, would feel compelled to put it the other way around.

How many men have a tendency to think of their wives as

something *owned*? They feel justified in exerting total control, sometimes even over matters that should be the exclusive domain of their wives, and to live their lives more or less as if their wives did not exist.

Consider, for example, this true account:

My Uncle Tony came to this country from Italy in the twenties with a young wife, my Aunt Carmella, but with very few material goods. He found jobs in motion picture theaters, which were just getting started, and which were then called "photo plays" and eventually, "movies." Sound films, or "talkies," had not yet been invented.

My aunt and uncle were poor, but, nevertheless, they saved enough to move to the Catskills. Eventually Uncle Tony had saved enough to buy a theater of his own. This was very lucky for him, because theaters were among the few businesses that flourished through the long depression that started at about that time. He prospered and bought more theaters, finally owning a string of six. Still, he and Aunt Carmella lived as frugally as before, and she had no idea of his burgeoning wealth. They lived all their lives in the same house he had bought when they moved from the city, and she either made her own clothes or bought cheap dresses. She was a simple, uneducated, and devoted wife, and the two of them lived essentially separate lives.

When Uncle Tony died, it was learned that he had left his entire fortune to Our Lady of Mount Carmel Church, except for a couple thousand dollars left to his brother. Aunt Carmella was stunned. She got nothing at all, except the house, and spent her last years impoverished and wretched. Uncle Tony, everyone said, had used his wealth to buy his way into heaven.

It would be difficult to find a more perfect example of marital infidelity, and yet, while this man's behavior evoked a great deal of comment in the community, there is no record of it being condemned by the church. In the unlikely event that his long-suffering wife had at any point in their dismal marriage gone to the arms of another man, however, then this would have been considered a clear case of infidelity.

There are numberless ways in which married partners can be faithless to each other that have nothing to do with sexual misconduct. Still, adultery cannot, in what has otherwise been a good and loving marriage, be taken lightly. It is probably the greatest threat a marriage can encounter. It is doubtful whether any passion matches in intensity the jealousy it evokes. It inflicts a wound that never really heals. A marriage that survives it is changed forever, and few indeed can survive such a stress.

We are here, of course, speaking of marriage in its true sense, a relationship based on love, not on convenience, legal documentation, or whatever. There is no doubt that some free spirits can treat infidelity lightly, as well as persons long separated who have never gotten around to divorce. These are not marriages in the sense at issue here.

Sexual jealousy appears to be more intense in men than in women. Some men have difficulty with the thought that their wives were sexually active before they even knew them, notwithstanding that this involves no threat to them whatsoever. A woman is less bothered by such thoughts, except, perhaps, for feeling that her husband has been immoral, which is very different from jealousy. Similarly, a man who has been, and perhaps still is, involved in a love affair is profoundly upset by the discovery that his wife is, too, perhaps from a desire to even the score, though he hardly has grounds for complaint.

Because of its destructive power, there are counselors who urge that a faithless partner not disclose to the other what has happened, and even to lie if asked, provided, of course, that the affair can be brought to a quiet end. But this is very dangerous ground and is, on its face, a dubious ethic. Whatever conditions in the marriage may have led to that behavior remain unresolved, and, worse, deception has low survival value. Sooner or later the truth comes out, and then the faithless spouse is twice damned—first as faithless, and then as a liar, who is likely never to be believed again.

Very often a husband or wife drifts to another person because something is missing in the marriage. Some men, to be sure, are inveterate womanizers, constantly on the lookout for sexual adventure notwithstanding a perfectly fulfilling marriage. In women this is quite rare; it is not so rare in men. A woman who discovers this, and is helpless to do anything about it, cannot possibly have a successful marriage, and divorce is the only way out. One can usually get over an injury, if the conditions are right, but you cannot get over one that is ongoing.

Usually, however, the fault is less with the faithless partner than with the marriage itself. A husband or wife is thus not so much lured into an affair as driven, and this provides reason for not automatically seeking divorce. What is missing in the marriage can, perhaps, be rectified, and that which is missing will be, once more, the fulfillment of needs, the very basis for love and fidelity. If that is the background for infidelity, then there might indeed be a better course of action than divorce, namely, an increased awareness and attentiveness on the part of the neglectful partner. This does sometimes happen. A man who has too long been absorbed in himself wakes up to what is wrong, and the couple can put the lapse of faith behind them. It will never be forgotten, but its destructive power can be minimized and the marriage reestablished.

Whether, in a given case, that is the correct diagnosis of the problem is at least worth considering before plunging into divorce proceedings, which are almost certain to yield an unhappy outcome. Adultery is commonly thought, with some justification, to be the ultimate betrayal of marriage, the crowning wrong. But it is not, as we have noted, the only kind of wrong. There are circumstances in which it is, from the standpoint of ethics, not considered to be the greatest wrong. Divorce law, in most jurisdictions, recognizes others.

The idea that divorce must be based upon someone's having done something is one that dies slowly, and this can turn a court hearing into a kind of charade. For example, a couple may simply decide that their marriage is unrewarding to both of them, and that it is time to go their separate ways. Neither wants to allege adultery, since none has occurred, so they decide to allege abuse, this being the least degrading of the grounds legally available. A liberal judge is not likely to insist upon much in the way of proof; what appears to be a bruise on the arm, for example, will suffice, and the divorce will be granted.

Adultery remains, however, the one universal ground for divorce, and the question arises, should it be alleged, assuming that this is not contested? Such an allegation is almost certain to produce warfare, which, while it will with certainty yield the divorce that is being sought, is still the worst way to achieve that end. A special opprobrium attaches to adultery, and someone hit with such a charge suffers a certain degree of disgrace, sometimes severely. Indeed, everyone is hurt—the defendant, the third party, and the plaintiff, too, in sometimes subtle ways. The knowledge that you have been betrayed by someone you trusted is not something to dwell upon.

For this reason, it will usually be best to avoid that accusation if possible, even if it can be proven, because even wars can sometimes be fought within certain restraints. Thus, an adulterous husband can be charged with "abandonment," for example, and a validly executed agreement of separation is apt to suffice for this. The divorced partners can then get on with their lives with some semblance of friendship, or, at least, mutual respect.

THE PENALTY FOR GUILT

A partner who undertakes to dissolve a marriage is likely to feel guilt, especially if the reason is involvement with a third person. This guilt is greatly intensified if children are involved and the marriage has been a long and seemingly stable one. The effect is apt to be a futile effort at friendship, and the consequences of this are almost always bad. For example:

We had been married for fifteen years and had two children. My wife seemed, to outsiders, the embodiment of what a wife should be. Our house was neat and immaculate, no magazine or dish was ever out of place, and she was herself the epitome of correctness. She dressed with taste and her behavior and manners were the perfect expression of propriety. No word ever left her lips which could not be uttered in the presence of a queen. It would be impossible to imagine her drunk, laughing loudly, or indulging in ribald humor. On top of all this, she was very pretty.

What was not apparent to others, however, was that she was, even in the privacy of our bed, stiff and prudish. Our days and nights together were always the same, always predictable, always cold, and boring. Still, I admired her for all her good qualities and accepted the marriage for what it was. I was myself very reserved, my work went well, our children thrived, and I had no thought of changing anything.

This all changed when my professional work took me to another city for a few months, my wife remaining at home with the children. There I was thrown in with people who were, to say the least, easy going, alive, and unconventional—free spirits. Parties with them were fun, and I was able to loosen up. There was nothing at all wrong with these people. They were all professionals like myself, respected by all, the difference being only that they had an enormous love of life. I spent many evenings with them, sometimes at their apartments, sometimes at their large and noisy parties, sometimes with one or two of them in a bar.

It wasn't long before I found myself getting involved with a female divorced member of this group, who was in basic ways the opposite of my wife. She was always sparkling, mischievous, and unconventional. She had a passion for sex, and for the first time in my life I knew what it was like to be totally alive in bed.

I returned home, drenched in shame and guilt. I somehow imagined that I could shed this through confession. So I gravely told my dutiful wife what had happened. I guess I thought that she would appreciate my contrition, forgive me, and we could then go back to our family life, though perhaps with a bit more warmth and love.

How stupid of me. The effect was not understanding (as though there was anything to "understand") but an explosion. Within a couple of days she had gone to a lawyer who set in motion the procedure for divorce. I engaged a lawyer for my own self-preservation, and soon I was receiving lengthy lists of outrageous "demands." I was made to feel like a criminal, and in fact, I somehow felt like one. I repeatedly offered to discuss everything with my wife, feeling sure that we could together arrive at a reasonable resolution of everything, but it was no use. The battle of the lawyers went on for over a year; costs, all borne by me, mounted alarmingly, and I finally agreed to a settlement that required nothing of her, but, along with much else, large support payments to her *for life.*

Several huge errors can be found in this account. The first is that the narrator allowed his intelligence to be overcome by guilt, which finally led him to accept highly one-sided terms of divorce. You simply cannot buy your way out of guilt by showering the person you have injured with gifts. Those support payments are, of course, still going on, and will, under normal circumstances, continue for a long time to come. They will not be appreciated, and they will not purchase any friendship or forgiveness; they will simply be accepted as due, and the lawyer who won them for her can congratulate himself on some fine lawyering.

The second mistake, of course, was the confession. Perhaps the truth had to come out sooner or later, but it should have waited until the marriage had been reestablished, so that the wife's security would seem less threatened.

And the third error was the husband's going to a lawyer. He should have passively resisted the whole procedure, agreeing to nothing, all the while displaying nothing but reasonableness and friendly feeling. A lawyer cannot compel you to respond. He can, of course, seek court orders, but a judge's sympathy is likely to tend toward the litigant who is attacked. Certainly engaging a lawyer should not be one's first response to an attack, and, in fact, it is the best way to get what you do *not* want.

chapter 4

dissolving the marriage

THE DIVORCE REVOLUTION

D ivorce has undergone revolutionary changes since the final decades of the twentieth century, both in the way people get divorced and the way divorce is thought of. That change continues and has, in fact, accelerated.

Divorce procedures were once entirely in the hands of lawyers. Divorce was an adversarial proceeding. One partner formally accused the other of wrongdoing, and the lawyer for that side undertook to prove it. Wrongdoing was variously defined in different jurisdictions, and sometimes limited to one thing, namely, adultery. The wrong was then conceived as a ground for dissolving the marriage, which was thought of as a kind of contract that has been breached. The guilty party was considered to some extent disgraced, and in some jurisdictions the degree of wrongdoing was reflected in the transfer of property, alimony, and custody of children. Such difficulties, and the sheer amount of time that it took to get a divorce, often forced people to seek divorce in distant jurisdictions, typically Nevada, sometimes Mexico.

We have, in a fairly brief time, moved so far from all this as to think of it as simply archaic and stupid. Laws themselves broke down. Someone could, for example, go to Alabama, stay overnight, pretending to be a resident in that jurisdiction, and for a large attorney's fee leave the next morning, the marriage dissolved. The make-believe and clear dishonesty became so obvious that radical change became necessary. Now one can, in almost every jurisdiction in this country, obtain a divorce under no-fault provisions or "irreconcilable differences." It is no longer necessary to prove wrongdoing, and divorced people suffer no shame or loss of reputation.

Divorce procedures are now rapidly catching up, although public awareness of this has been slow. Mediation is replacing adversarial proceedings. A large and growing class of professional mediators, dealing exclusively with divorce, has appeared, and is growing rapidly. Some of these mediators are attorneys who have rejected the adversarial role, but most are social workers, psychologists, and sometimes simply people who have set themselves up as divorce mediators, usually with special training from a self-governing mediation association of these. In addition, a growing number of accountants and financial advisors have moved into the field, calling themselves divorce specialists. These are likely to be sought when considerable wealth is at stake.

So the role of attorneys has in many cases been reduced almost to the vanishing point. Once a couple has, with the help of a mediator, arrived at a formal agreement on such things as division of property, custody of children, and so on, then only one lawyer is needed, to submit the agreement to a court of law, to be embodied in a decree of divorce. No one needs to appear in court, and the lawyer's role is hardly more than clerical. Sometimes, however, a mediator will insist, as a final step, that there be two lawyers, one for each partner, to review the agreement and ensure that fairness has been achieved. This is by no means necessary. Indeed, going even further, a couple, provided they are cooperative and have no desire for battle, can now draw up their own agreement, without assistance even from a mediator, and hand this agreement over to a single attorney, who then files it with the court. This is, of course, not without risks, and requires a great deal of goodwill and cooperation.

The decline of the role of lawyers in divorce proceedings has thus resulted in an ever-increasing number of divorces being mediated. Mediation, however, does not mean the same thing to all mediators, but can take a variety of forms.

So if we classify the different ways that a marriage can be dissolved, there turn out to be, very roughly, five, from the very worst to the very best. Unfortunately, the worst is still the most common, because the others are likely to be unknown, but also because the breakup of a marriage tends to bring out the belligerence of the parties. The fifth and best way is rare indeed, precisely because it requires the parties to completely set aside any tendency toward belligerence.

The five ways are:

1. **War:** Bitterly contested litigation involving attorneys for each side and aiming at victory for one but usually resulting in defeat for both.
2. **Arbitration:** Putting the otherwise contentious decisions in the hands of a third, neutral party.
3. **Standard mediation:** Engaging a third person to work out an agreement in the shadow of the law, in the presence of the two parties, but in the absence of attorneys.
4. **Open mediation:** Engaging a third person to help the two parties negotiate an agreement acceptable to both and placing their needs above considerations of legal entitlement.
5. **Rational and amicable settlement:** Omitting both lawyers and mediators so that the two parties can work out their own terms in a spirit of cooperation.

These will be explained and illustrated in turn, to show the pitfalls and disastrous consequences of pursuing the first, and still typical, approach, and the advantages of the others. Which method is used depends primarily on the temperaments of the divorcing couple. Divorce, while not uncommon, is still not a common occurrence in the lives of most people (the occasional exception usually being celebrities). People thus tend to assume that it is accomplished only through adversarial proceeding. Not long ago this was indeed true, but no longer.

FIRST LEVEL: WARFARE

As we have noted, human beings tend to think in terms of absolutes, and nowhere is this more true than with respect to marriage. You're either married or you're not. Even if a man has been long separated from his wife, and the marriage is in every sense dead, there is an approbrium attached to his becoming involved with another woman, and she, in particular, is likely to feel uncomfortable about it. She is likely to be advised not even to see him; he is, after all, a married man. And the same applies, of course, to a woman.

So it is widely supposed that, since one acquires this special and unique status of being a married person, the only way to shed that status is to get a divorce. This is the almost spontaneous thinking of most people, expressed as either/or. If a woman discovers that her husband is involved in an affair, her immediate thought is likely to be to divorce him. If a man finds himself deeply unhappy in his marriage, his thoughts, too, turn at once to divorce. And what happens at that point? You turn to a lawyer, to initiate the necessary steps. This is so common that it seems almost routine in failing marriages. It does not occur to people that there are other, better ways to dissolve a marriage.

Litigation is usually the worst possible way, short of murder. It is the most bitter kind of litigation that lawyers deal with. Couples who were once in love and, until recently, may have gone about things with the minimum of friction, quite suddenly turn into implacable foes. Each is more intent upon inflicting woe on the other than in finding a way out of the unhappiness. Of course, not all divorce proceedings go this way, but they typically do, more or less. Divorcing couples usually have little that is good to say about each other.

Why is this so? Why do people who were once in love, people who solemnly vowed to love each other forever, so often become the bitterest of enemies? Here we are not asking why marriages fail with such regularity; that is a large question, dealt with elsewhere. Instead we ask: Why all the anger when they do fail?

The anger exists because the grown-ups involved simply revert to being children. We have all seen how children act. One pushes, the other pushes back, the resentment builds, each retaliation becoming worse than the last until and unless a grown-up intercedes, real injury can result. It is a kind of behavior that comes with being a child, and it takes great parental skill and patience to counteract it. The right to retaliate seems to any child like a given: "Why did you hit him?" "Because he hit me!"

This is the psychology of divorcing people. If they encounter each other in a crowd, they turn away, as if strangers. They engage lawyers to do their hitting for them. Friends feel embarrassment if they find themselves in the presence of both; it is just assumed that they hate each other. If they go to a family mediator to try to work out an agreement, they generally try not to speak to each other.

This is all extremely silly, obviously, and one wonders how grown people could regress to such behavior. Of course not all people do, but it is nonetheless common, and those who do not are likely to have to struggle with themselves to avoid it. The reasons for this are not difficult to see.

The first is that adult behavior is something learned, and it does not come easily. There is always the child within us, pulling us back, and under stress, we yield.

Additionally, divorce is a severe blow to one's self-esteem, the more so when some third person is involved. Someone has cast you aside. You are seen to be worth less than you deserve. You have been abandoned. If in the face of this you are able to smile, then it is a brave smile, an act, meant to conceal your inward sense of rejection. So you become very angry.

And, of course, quite apart from psychological factors, divorce represents a real threat to things that are of indisputable importance—your basic security, your relationship with your children, and so on. And when threatened, people strike out, often irrationally.

So as soon as one partner to a marriage engages a lawyer to commence divorce proceedings, the other partner engages one, too, to protect his or her interests, which means, ultimately, to fight back. A sense of threat hangs over everything. Each is apt to feel that there is someone out there, a smart attorney, set upon getting him or her. The seeds of all the anger and bitterness that typically accompany divorce are now ready to be nourished.

An attorney's job is to get the best deal possible for the client, no matter the expense to the other partner. That other partner has a defender, too, the other lawyer, whose aim is the same, to get the best deal possible. Any lawyer, to the extent that this is achieved, and at whatever expense to others, is considered to be doing a good, lawyerly job. In the event that the client still harbors a residue of friendship and respect for the other partner, then the lawyer has no interest in encouraging it. This was illustrated by a wife who thought she might be entitled to some of the pension that had been earned by her husband, but she was reluctant to press this, feeling that it was he who had earned it and that his financial situation would suffer considerably if much of it was taken away from him. Her attorney's advice was: "Don't feel sorry for him."

The battle between a divorcing couple, in effect directed from opposite corners of the ring by their attorneys, thus takes on the form of a tug of war. The attorneys themselves appear to be bitter foes, and their communications with each other will typically reflect this, consisting of demands, thinly disguised (never open) threats, and so on, as if each were thinking of himself as the force of good battling the forces of evil. This is the way the game is played. The two attorneys might, in fact, be good friends, golf partners, or whatever, and litigants are apt to be astonished if, perchance, they discover this. A lawyer's behavior, while fighting for the client, might appear fierce indeed, as if aimed at ripping the other attorney to shreds, but this need not interfere with the golf game they have planned for the next day.

The bitterness of the divorcing couple, however, is very real, and nourished by fear that easily rises to paranoia. Deep hatred soon takes hold. Friendship, or even civility, becomes impossible. Friends, and lovers, are easily turned into enemies, and enemies, once blows have been struck, can never restore that friendship. Hatred is a powerful force, while love is a weak one by comparison.

On top of the destructive feelings thus engendered there are the measurable costs of attorneys fees, sometimes huge ones, and these, again, nourish even further feelings of resentment.

Along the way there is likely to be much maneuvering and attempts at deception, especially with respect to ownership of property. Each sees the other lawyer as an ever-present threat, and his or her own lawyer as a kind of shield. It can become costly in terms of sleep, and at times even health.

Costs and anger grow with each new legal tactic. A "retainer" is demanded; that is, an advance fee, often very large, providing the attorney with some assurance that he will not be dropped in favor of some other lawyer. "Discovery" proceedings are initiated, compelling a spouse to disclose certain documents, such as tax returns, ownership of property, bank accounts, and the like. "Depositions" are taken; that is, sworn testimony in writing from third parties who might know something that would be damning to one of the other parties in the divorce, such as adultery, drug use, physical abuse, psychological problems, and so on. Detailed inventories are demanded of things owned, even things of trivial value that the husband, for example, has always thought of as indisputably his.

It can all become unbelievably messy, and the passage of time often just exacerbates things. Soon the divorcing parties refuse to speak to each other, or even look at each other, so despised has each become in the eyes of the other. Children are likely to be used as weapons, one partner attempting to minimize the other's contact with them. An attempt is sometimes even made to poison the children's minds against the other parent. And of course the wounds inflicted by all the warfare never heal. After the divorce has been granted the children are passed back and forth under the "visitation" rights imposed by the court's decrees. And perhaps the saddest part of all is that the children are likely, over time, to take sides, to the extent that they can become totally estranged from one or the other parent. And the scars on them will never really heal, for this is the image of marriage that they will bring to their own marriages.

No one ever wins such a war, except the attorneys, whose fees grow with every hurdle. Things are never settled to the satisfaction of both parties. Everything from property arrangements to custodial provisions will be the result of compromise. Someone has to give up something precious in order to get something else. And both parties, once deeply in love and believing in love everlasting, are instead infected forever with profound hatred for each other.

There are even divorced couples who carry on their warfare long after a divorce is granted, seizing upon opportunities to injure the other, every blow struck by one side producing retaliation on the other. For example, the man knowing that his former wife depends for her water supply on a well that is located in land he owns cuts off the supply. Or the ex-husband possesses the deed to the property they jointly own, half of which she is now entitled to. So he holds the document under lock until he has wrung a perhaps meaningless concession from her—for example, forcing her to compose a written apology for some claimed injury. Or again, a former wife claims that the father of her young son is a pedophile, and teaches the child to declare this as well. A divorced man buys property, for which he has no other use, adjoining his former wife's home, with the view to finding ways to reduce her property value, or otherwise harass her.

Of course the reliable effect of such pointless harassment is retaliation. A person dealt such a blow usually has weapons of his or her own with which to strike back, and an attorney can often supply even more. The battle thus feeds upon itself, and there is no turning back. Is it childish behavior? Of course. But these are only a few of the actual experiences of divorced people I have known.

Bitterness between divorcing couples is much magnified when large amounts of money are involved. This is always the danger faced by men whose businesses or professions have gained them great wealth and who then marry women of slight means. The thinking of such men is sometimes that their bride, if she is a stunning beauty but of humble origin and status and little material means, will bask in her husband's glory and that he will thus be rewarded with lasting devotion. It is, in short, an ego trip for him. He wins an expensive trophy. Of course such a marriage, based upon little that is of significance, is fragile indeed, and when it fails, her attorney has every inducement to go after his wealth, no holds barred. It is the stuff of the popular media.

The other exacerbating factor is young children. Custody was once almost routinely awarded to the mother, but this is no longer so, and the groundwork is laid for fierce battle. Each of the partners is faced with the challenge, not only to prove his or her parental virtues, but to diminish the other's. Property can be divided, but children cannot. Custody and visitation rights must be fought over, and those most injured are always, of course, the children, the spoils of this warfare.

And here again are planted the seeds of further discord, each being tempted to turn the children against the other. The children are thus led to take sides, and not only the children but also the losing parent is forever injured. So is the one who "wins."

It is bad enough when children have to live with parental warfare, but it is worse when such warfare continues beyond the divorce. A parent is almost never denied visitation rights by the court, no matter what faults may be alleged by the other parent, and the scheduled exchange of the children normally brings these parents face-to-face. Shouting breaks out and often physical abuse, witnessed by the children. Some judges, rightly concerned about the effects on the children, order that they be exchanged in some designated public place at designated days and times, the idea being that warfare is less likely to break out in such a setting. This very often does not work—the parents fight anyway, not only in front of the children, but also in public. To counteract this one judge created an arrangement under which the parents would not need even to see each other. Two adjoining rooms were set aside at a counseling center, supplied with toys, and the parents were ordered to arrive there at staggered times. The parent having the children then deposited them in the care of an approved security person at one of the rooms; the other parent arrived afterward at the adjoining room, where the children were turned over. At the end of the visitation the same arrangement is repeated, in reverse. Visitation rights are thus protected, the warring parents are spared the sight of each other, and the children are spared the dreadful sight of battle.

Since its inception, this arrangement has been picked up by other family courts. Where the security personnel are under salary, the costs are borne by the family court, but the rooms, used exclusively for this purpose, are often provided at no cost by some nonprofit organization. Costs paid by the court—that is, by the taxpayers—actually represent money saved, because of the reduction of ongoing lawsuits otherwise fought by the parents.

Of course involving attorneys in divorce proceedings does not always have such baneful consequences, but they are common enough that divorce as battle is almost the general conception. Divorced people generally do not like each other. The reason is that they are cast as belligerents where real and sometimes huge loss is threatened. And such belligerence is almost always exacerbated by the involvement of lawyers. This does not mean that lawyers are dishonorable people. It is simply the result of casting divorce into an adversarial role where it doesn't really belong at all. But that is the setting that lawyers are trained to deal with. It is always X versus Y, two opposed sides, and each attorney's aim is to be on the winning side. Lawyers are not to blame for the warfare. They fill a necessary role. When someone wants war, then he or she needs all the help that can be found for waging it. It is the parents who are at fault. Battle, while it may be a common result of being human, is not a necessary one. It is precipitated largely by the inability of some couples to simply grow up.

SECOND LEVEL: ARBITRATION

Divorce by arbitration involves replacing battling attorneys with an arbiter, whose task is to weigh the issues on both sides and then arrive at a compromise acceptable, or at least not totally unacceptable, to both sides. This largely removes the temptation to dissimulate, as warring partners must almost always do. The arbiter sees both sides and instead of trying to win something for one side at the expense of the other, tries to satisfy both at the least cost.

This is a tried-and-true method of settling certain kinds of disputes, such as those between labor and management. Sometimes warring parties are forced by law or contract to turn to arbitration. It also works well for minor disputes, and many communities have dispute-resolution centers based on arbitration. Suppose, for example, that someone wants to cut some of the limbs from a tree growing in his neighbor's yard, but which overhang and darken his property. The neighbor objects. There are no laws concerning such a situation, and it would be impractical to go to court over the matter. Something like this is appropriately turned over to an arbiter, agreed to by the disputing parties, who may agree in advance to abide by the arbiter's decision.

Such a model does not work for marital disputes, simply

because the stakes are too high, and neither party is willing to surrender control to an outsider. It should be noted, however, that at the point where matters involving or arising from a divorce proceeding arrive in court, before a judge, the judge becomes in effect an arbiter, whom the parties have no voice in selecting, and his or her decision is binding. This is especially true when the dispute involves children.

This is something a litigant is likely to learn with shock and dismay. In cases like this judges have vast power, and vast discretion. Divorce proceedings present an enormous variety of problems; no two are quite alike. Statuary law, accordingly, cannot cover all of these potential variables, and matters are left to judicial discretion, which can sometimes seem capricious. Still, once the judge has spoken, the matter is closed. Here is an example:

> Soon after we were divorced my former husband moved to a distant city, leaving me with custody of our very young daughter. He almost never saw her and evidently had little desire to, having remarried and started a new family. It seemed to me that our daughter had little reason to retain his surname, since I had reverted to my maiden name, so I sought permission to change her name to mine. Her father had no objection, so it seemed like a foregone conclusion. We presented the request to the judge, who of course did not know us and had no real understanding of the situation. To my astonishment, he ruled against me, declaring that it "would not be in the best interest of the child." No reason at all was given for that opinion, but, as my lawyer said, "The ball game is over." There are no replays in matters like this.

It is worth noting that this mother had other means for effecting a name change. She was but another victim of the notion that, if you have what appears to be a legal problem, you should go to a lawyer. Thus, if her daughter was prekindergarten, the mother needed only to register her in school under the preferred name. Schools do not require parents to prove who their children are when they bring them in. Her husband was far away and evidently would not have objected. This would have resulted in the child being known to all by the preferred name for the next twelve years, and indeed beyond, for a college would have no reason to question the name on her school records. If, on the other hand, the child was already in school under the original name, the mother could simply have asked that it be changed on their records. If the father then objected and that did not work, then there still remain other options. For example, the mother could take out a custodial account for her daughter under the preferred name. At the point when the child should begin to have an income, from whatever source, even if modest, and an income tax return would need to be filed, then it could be filed under the preferred name. Tax records could then be presented to a social security office, so that her social security number would correspond with the new name. Eventually a driver's permit would be sought, and with these records the daughter's photo identification would bear the desired name, and that would, for all intents and purposes, be an end to the matter.

Of course this somewhat complex maneuvering might not work in the end, but chances are it would, and, in any case, the mother would have at least some control, rather than surrendering it all to a total stranger in the robes of a judge.

Here is another example of judicial discretion:

> I had agreed to rather generous support payments to my wife in the course of negotiating the terms of a divorce, and then learned that she had received a large inheritance from an aunt. It was clear to me that she no longer needed payments of such magnitude from me, so I petitioned the court to have them reduced, submitting the amount of the inheritance for his consideration. To my astonishment he, apparently without even considering the inheritance, and perhaps not even knowing what it was, just said, "let's set this aside and see what it is that you are paying." He thereby simply disregarded the entire basis for my bringing the proceeding, and left everything just as it was. But I couldn't challenge it.

Sometimes a judge will decide that not only the statutes pertaining to divorce are flawed, but that established precedents also need improving, in which case he or she might, entirely on judicial authority, make up his or her own rules to fit the situation. These may have no basis whatever, except the judge's own judgment or wisdom, but still, such rules, once applied to a given case, are binding.

Property settlements, for example, typically distinguish between marital and nonmarital, or "extra," property, the latter being property inherited by one of the partners, or property owned or earned prior to the marriage. This is traditionally deemed to belong to the partner who received it, and thus beyond the reach of the other.

One family court judge of long experience, however, decided that this was one-sided, so he invented a new rule. He decided that 5 percent of such property should be absorbed as marital property during each year of the marriage following its receipt, so that after twenty years it will cease to have the special status of nonmarital property and may be considered to belong to both. In the event that the marriage should fail before twenty years, then only as much of the property shall be set aside as marital property as remains, after deducting 5 percent of it for each year that the marriage survived after the property was first received.

That fairly complex rule was, clearly, the invention of a single judge, acting from a discretion that is often allowed to judges, but it took hold, and, eventually, other courts within the state started applying the same rule. In other words, it became a precedent, though not necessarily one that was binding on other judges but a decision that could be used to support similar decisions in the future.

When a divorce is bitterly contested and disputes keep arising, then matters, left largely to the discretion of the judge, can become very complex and unpredictable, costing great sums of money and much sleep. Confronted with the power of judges, one needs a very resourceful (and expensive) attorney.

Here is an example:

Under the divorce decree I was obligated to pay 15 percent of the income from my medical practice to my wife, for support, plus another 15 percent to each of our children until they reached eighteen years of age. All other income, from investments or whatever, was excluded. Thirty-seven years later I retired, and since I no longer had any income from medical practice, the support payments stopped. Four years later she learned that I had a substantial pension, and brought a court action to obtain 15 percent of that, retroactive, plus another 15 percent for each of the children, the youngest of which was now in his thirties and, of course, entirely independent. The family court ruled against her, but that did not end things. She appealed all the way to the state appellate court, beyond which I would have no further recourse. Her attorney was given thirty days to file the details of her claim. Thirty-four days came and went, and I thought, with great relief, that the battle was finally over, by default. The appellate court, however, decided to disregard that limitation, and I was left to anguish for the next eighteen months, when the matter finally came to trial. The judges gave us just five minutes each to state our positions, and then ruled against her. But by that time I had spent another fifteen thousand dollars on attorney's fees and had been forced to make many trips to the distant city where the court sat, not to mention the pall that was cast over my life by eighteen months of anxious waiting.

There are several lessons to be gleaned from this appalling account. First, we see again the vast power of judges, and the seemingly arbitrary choices they can make with respect to a litigant, sometimes at enormous cost, both material and emotional. This physician spent a year and a half waiting for a precious five minutes before the court. The court itself had no compunction about disregarding the thirty-day rule, which the petitioner had every reason to think had settled things.

Second, we see lawyering at its typical worst. Here, in total disregard of fairness, the opposing attorney went all out to grab from the respondent everything that was remotely possible, including a claim for children now long grown up. This he considered his role, as lawyers normally do, leaving it to the other side to erect whatever defenses it could.

And finally, we see again the towering cost of such warfare. The physician had, by this time, no choice, being up against a resourceful attorney and his resolute client, but the account does drive home the need, if at all possible, to avoid litigation in dissolving the marriage in the first place. Everyone loses, often heavily—except, of course, the attorneys.

Courts, in dealing with problems of domestic relations, always have one paramount rule, and that is to try to serve the interests of any children involved. It has thus been aptly said that every child has three parents—mother, father, and the state. This third parent is, of course, quite willing to stay out of things so long as the child's well-being is not in question, but when it is, the court steps in with a very heavy hand indeed, and one that cannot, for all practical purposes, be challenged.

The results are sometimes astonishing. For example, more than one divorced husband has found himself obligated to provide support for children that are not even his. This has been the outcome of sophisticated DNA tests fairly recently developed. Thus, a divorced father learns, from such testing, that one or more of the small children, now in the custody of his former wife, were not fathered by him, and that he was deluded into thinking they were his during the marriage. Now he quite understandably sees no reason why he should be held responsible for their support. Let it be the responsibility of the faithless wife, or the biological father. The court nevertheless holds that the petitioner must pay, and there is not a thing he can do about it except to protest. He will be their support until they reach eighteen. Some states, to be sure, exempt divorced men from such an obligation by statute, but many do not. It is left to the discretion of the judge, who, in the child's interest, is likely to disregard the very understandable feelings of the ex-husband. And in fact, in at least one case, a judge compelled an ex-husband to provide such support payments even where an actual statute exempted him. This was a case in which, with his consent, his wife bore a child that had been artificially conceived, using an anonymous donor.

What is the lesson to be gleaned from all this? It is to avoid if possible the kind of binding arbitration that results from putting matters in the hands of a judge. You surrender all semblance of control at that point, and can walk out of the court with a bitter pill to swallow. There is almost never any point in appealing a judge's decision, for appellate courts are reluctant to wade into a domestic dispute that has already been competently, albeit it unfairly, dealt with.

THIRD LEVEL: STANDARD MEDIATION

Divorce mediation is of quite recent origin. It began when an attorney, knowing the typically destructive effects of litigation, undertook to represent *both* husband and wife in their effort to reach a settlement, thus taking the side of neither. He found that this worked well, and so abandoned the adversarial approach altogether. He was at first roundly rebuked by the legal profession, his new approach being seriously at odds with what had become established as a basic tenet of legal ethics; namely, to do all that you can for your client, in the expectation that "the other side" will be similarly represented by another attorney. Even to take into account the interests of the opposing party, thereby weakening your ability to represent the interests of your own client, was thought of as not fulfilling your obligation to the person who hired you, a conflict of interest.

That is still the way most lawyers think with respect to divorce proceedings. If, for example, your wife is seeking a divorce and has engaged an attorney to represent her, and you, seeking to simplify matters and perhaps save on legal fees, call upon that attorney to help you *both*, you will be instructed that he, the attorney, cannot represent both plaintiff and defendant at the same time, and will feel free to use any information that you give him to bolster his client's case. It is the lawyer's duty, as an attorney, to cut the very best deal he can for his client. To get your own best deal possible, hire your own attorney.

Of course none of this applies to the so-called uncontested divorce. Here one partner (the "plaintiff") files for divorce and the other (the "defendant") does not contest the action. Termination of the marriage then requires little more than what amounts to a clerical action on the part of just one attorney; that is, he files the documentation with the court. This can happen when the partners are young, without children, and without significant property. They simply decide to go their separate ways. Lawyers sometimes advertise fixed, low fees for handling such divorces.

Divorce settlements that are arrived at through mediation also amount to uncontested divorces. In these cases, such matters as custody of children, visitation rights, allotment of properties, and so on are arrived at through negotiation with the help of one mediator, who need not be, and usually is not, an attorney.

Today a growing number of accountants and financial planners are assuming the role of "divorce specialists," whose function is to sort out the sometimes complex matters of ownership presented by the warring parties. They are in a position to determine just who should get what, and since they have and understand objective standards for determining this, their decisions are likely to be accepted. Their role, however, is limited to cases in which large and complex property claims are at stake. They are not in any position to decide such matters as custody of children, visitation rights, and so on. So, their services are important to a rather limited clientele, and they by no means meet the needs of most people.

The best way for most persons seeking to dissolve their marriages is through mediation, which resembles traditional arbitration in some ways, but still enables the divorcing couple to retain some control when done properly.

What is not generally known is that there are different approaches to divorce mediation. There is no set procedure, and some ways of doing it are clearly better than others, although much depends on the attitudes and temperaments of the couples seeking it. Mediators who were trained as lawyers are likely to do things differently than those trained as social workers or psychologists, for example. A very considerable literature on mediation has appeared in the past several years, and almost any library has several books on the subject. What follows will not be a comprehensive coverage, but rather a general description, concentrating on the things that divorcing couples should focus on.

What is common to all divorce mediation is that the mediator is supposed to make none of the decisions. All she can do is suggest trade-offs; the decisions are, in the end, supposed to be made jointly by the divorcing couple. They can be very difficult, for example, where children are involved, but, to the extent that the mediation process succeeds, no one is compelled to do anything. Even when the outcome is not what one would have wanted, it is at least one that was agreed to, however reluctantly. It will in any case be better than something that was forced on both parties by a judge.

Mediation is thus the very opposite of litigation. The latter is a tug of war, with attorneys serving as surrogates for the divorcing couple and supplying some of the weapons. A mediator, on the other hand, instead of expending energy to win from an adversary, tries to reach a common goal wherein *both* can win. A lawyer considers that she has done her job well to the extent that she was able to turn aside the demands of the other and gain the maximum awards for her client, even at the other's expense and with little concern for fairness, whereas the mediator's job is to satisfy, to the extent possible, the needs of both parties.

The increase of mediation over litigation has resulted, not only from the inappropriateness of the former, but also from the increased incidence of divorce. Opprobrium was once attached to divorce, so that a man's reputation was tarnished. No divorced man, it was thought, could offer himself as a candidate for the presidency of the United States, for example. Divorce was even prohibited in some jurisdictions, and made difficult everywhere. Divorcing couples had to resort to subterfuge, moving temporarily to another jurisdiction, such as Nevada, and pretending to intend permanent residence. And a divorced woman was thought a kind of reject, with a seriously compromised chance of ever remarrying. Very little of these attitudes remain today, and even evangelical religions, which place great emphasis on family values, do not for the most part condemn divorce. It is just too common.

The other factor giving rise to the growth of mediation is, of course, the sheer unpleasantness of engaging in prolonged battle with someone who was loved, plus the often high cost of hiring lawyers.

In any case, divorce mediation is a flourishing and growing profession. There is a large professional network, distributing literature and news to members, and regular courses, often under the aegis of a university. In one large American city (Rochester, New York) over 25 percent of divorces are dealt with by mediation.

There are two general approaches to divorce mediation, which I shall somewhat arbitrarily call "standard mediation" and "open mediation." In standard mediation the mediator essentially does the work of attorneys, and is governed by an objective standard, namely, divorce law. She in effect does the work of two attorneys, one for each side, although no attorneys are involved during the mediation process. They are, however, waiting in the wings, so to speak, one for each side, whose responsibility will be to examine the agreement finally hammered out, each then satisfying themselves that the interests of their clients have been met. This will normally involve at least one conference, but it need not. To the extent that the attorneys have anything to do with the mediation, which will usually be very little, they deal with the mediator. There is, then, a collaboration between mediator and attorneys, arranged in advance. Indeed, the mediator will have sought them out for this purpose, and the arrangement between a mediator and the two attorneys is ongoing. Then, as agreements are reached through mediation, one or the other of the attorneys will file the necessary documents, incorporating the agreement, with the court. This is done for one pair of clients after another, for a set, customary fee.

There are several advantages to this kind of mediation, for everyone concerned—for the divorcing couple, for the mediator, and for the lawyers. Thus, the lawyers receive a decent but not excessive fee for what amounts to a routine, fairly simple procedure—checking over the agreement and filing it with the court. The mediator, who does virtually all of the professional work, is paid appropriately by the parties involved, her hourly charges usually being adjusted to the resources of the divorcing parties. And, most important, the divorcing couple achieves great savings in both time and money. In addition, mediation minimizes the potential for warfare, since the couple meets together in the presence of the mediator, who can usually keep a lid on emotions.

The amount of money saved is considerable, first, because the mediator's hourly charge will be far less, probably less than half, of what each of the two attorneys' fees would be, and second, because negotiations move along much faster than they do when attorneys negotiate, often endlessly, with each other, and consult in the meantime with their clients. Normally it will take less than half as many meetings with a mediator than with an attorney.

What does the mediator do in these proceedings? She does the work of the attorneys, in effect, sitting in for both of them, making sure that each party gets what is allowable by law, and for the rest, seeking common ground from the couple, with respect to what each wants and what each is willing to give.

Thus, the law is likely to require that marital property must be divided in some way, and further, that "extramarital property" not be subject to negotiation. Property acquired during the marriage includes such things as savings, investments from income earned, pension benefits, and so on. These are treated as joint property, to which each has legitimate claim.

The concept of property jointly owned is a reflection of the view that marriage is a partnership, and while the roles of the married partners may differ, one of them gaining the income while the other does most of the parenting, for example, they share equally in the material rewards of that partnership. For example, let us suppose that, during the marriage, the husband assembled a valuable collection of books. Even though his wife may have no interest in these, they are joint property, and if the matter were left to a judge, he might insist that they be sold and the proceeds divided, since the value of the collection would be seriously degraded by simply dividing them. A lawyer, knowing this, might take the same approach. And a mediator, trying to reach a settlement under the guidance of this principle, would at least to some extent be bound by this, too. She would not feel free to simply insist that the books go to the husband.

The mediator, can, however, suggest a trade-off. For example, if it should turn out that the wife has, for example, assembled a collection of old quilts, in which the husband has no interest, then the mediator would suggest that the books go to the husband and the quilts to the wife, without any consideration of their relative value.

Similarly, with regard to household furnishings. If these were purchased during the marriage, then in principle they belong to both. But a mediator can suggest that they both go through them, indicating which pieces the wife wants, which the husband wants, which both want, and which neither wants. The effect is to narrow negotiation down to the third category, and trade-offs would again be in order. Dickering of this sort is much more effectively carried on between the two parties under the guidance of a mediator than by two attorneys exchanging demands, the litigants meanwhile digging in their heels at every point. The real problems arise, of course, with things of great value that cannot be simply divided, swapped, or sold, most typically real estate and children.

Suppose, for example, that both want the house, and neither has an absolute claim to it. Here the mediator has a great advantage over a pair of sparring lawyers, for she can kick it around with both parties at once, searching for avenues of compromise. The resolution of this would perhaps await the resolution of problems regarding custody of children, the house going to whichever parent is given custody. Or perhaps one spouse could purchase the other's equity in the house. The mediator, under this standard approach, would have to give due consideration to the rights of each parent, but could help them negotiate compromises, rather than having two lawyers pulling in opposite directions.

Retirement benefits can pose serious problems, but under what we are calling standard mediation, there are objective ways of resolving them. Typically the husband, if he has been the main source of income, will regard these benefits as his, since it is he who has earned them. The matter can be especially sticky if he is far from retirement age. Still, since these benefits are something of value that were acquired during the marriage, then in some jurisdictions the wife, as full partner in marriage, has equal claim to them. The matter becomes even more complicated if some of these benefits were earned prior to the marriage and some after, and sometimes the manner of distributing such benefits, upon retirement, can be complex and time-related, complicating things still further.

The mediator's task in this case is to invoke mathematical formulas, sometimes of an arcane nature, to arrive at the division that, under law, will be required. Still, complex as these calculations may become, it is far better, for all concerned, that they be in the hands of one person than that lawyers, with perhaps very different interpretations of the factors involved, should be trying to resolve them.

The legal guidelines that are applied to what we are calling standard mediation are obviously valuable in some cases. This kind of mediation does have one great problem, however, and that is, that what the law requires is not always what ordinary fairness would dictate.

Consider, for example, the requirement that pension benefits earned during the marriage must be shared. The presupposition that each partner has, in his or her own way, contributed to these, can be quite false. Suppose, for example, that the husband is, from the stand-point of his employer, the owner of this pension, and that he is also the primary parent, the wife having full-time work that provides no pension. The partnership is clearly one-sided, yet the law does not take this into account, and the husband is understandably resentful.

Or consider the rule of extramarital property. Let us suppose that the property was bestowed upon the wife by inheritance. This can have the consequence that her needs are more or less met by her independent wealth. If the husband is nevertheless obligated to render generous support payments to her or the children, or to entitle her to half of his pension benefits years in advance of when they will be drawn, then obviously the two are not being dealt with equitably.

The following illustrates this problem:

> My wife had, in her name, considerable wealth, which she inher-ited before we got married, and she kept it intact, rarely drawing on it to meet daily household expenses or unusual costs. She really did not need much of my income, and yet, considering it my traditional responsibility to provide the support of the family, I bore the weight of the expenses. When we broke up, we went to mediation, where it seemed obvious to me that, if I were no longer going to be her husband, these responsibilities could to some extent be shed and, in particular, that she would have no need for my pension benefits. But the mediator would not allow us to consider that. He claimed that all this was governed by law. I could not believe it had to be that way, so he insisted that I con-sult an attorney on my own, for verification. I did that, and to my astonishment, he agreed with the mediator. Maybe this was better than throwing the whole problem to attorneys or putting it before a judge, but the advantage did not seem to be all that great.

Often the mediator's greatest challenge will arise when chil-dren, especially very young children, are involved. Although there is still a presumption on the part of many judges that custody should go to the mother, exceptions are increasingly made. The days when the father was the breadwinner and the mother the homemaker are long gone. Two-income households are common, as more and more women enter business and the professions. In some cases there has been a complete role reversal, the father becoming a "house husband" while mother pursues her profession.

Still the assignment of custody is usually difficult, on top of which is the extremely difficult matter of visitation rights. One parent is almost certain to feel reduced to second-class status. Here divorce law is apt to supply no certain guide, and matters must be worked out between the parties, with the help of the mediator. Every case will be different, and almost certainly difficult. The advantage over litigation is still apparent, however. The parents are much more likely to be spared the wrenching roles of fighting over the children.

But sometimes this approach can produce absurd results. For example, the law might assume that one will be the custodial parent and that the other will be responsible for child support, and it may even require documentation to this effect. But what if the custodial parent turns out to be the father, and the only one with a regular and ample income? Or what if the two want to share custody, in a way that seems reasonable to both but which is not reflected in the law? For example, the law is likely to recognize *divided* custody, but leave no room for *shared* custody. The law is likely to rest on the assumption that the children will "live with" one parent, that is, the custodial parent, and "visit" the other according to a prearranged schedule. But what if the parents remain neighbors, and the children go back and forth more or less at will? With whom do they live?

These are obstacles that the mediator and clients must somehow overcome, creating at least the appearance of following the law, and in the hope that the two lawyers, who will review the agreement before submitting it to a judge for approval, will not at the last minute cause difficulty.

Now the question arises as to why, if this is how mediation works, should anyone turn to it, if the mediator is simply a surrogate for the lawyers and if the outcome is going to be much the same as if everything were handled by them from the start. The answer is that it saves time and money and usually reduces emotional tension. Instead of paying two lawyers, often over the course of many months, and wondering what they might be coming up with, you pay one mediator, and you know at every meeting just how things are going. And while opposing lawyers are likely, or almost certain, to make excessive demands, which have to be whittled down, the mediator makes no demands at all, but instead weighs the actual interests and entitlements of both partners.

The one set of circumstances in which such standard mediation works best is when the two parties are in a litigious, rather than a cooperative, frame of mind. Even in mediation, where this is discouraged, the two parties might be trying, each of them, to get everything they can with only minimal consideration of the needs of the other. In this case they can be presented with certain rules, drawn from the law or precedent, to which they must yield. Neither party, for example, could demand a share of the extramarital property of the other, no matter how fair or reasonable that might seem. Guidelines settle the matter, and adversarial impulses are kept in check.

FOURTH LEVEL: OPEN MEDIATION

While divorce mediation began as a specialty within the legal profession, it is now by no means limited to attorneys. Social workers and psychologists have moved into the field in great numbers. In fact, in most states *anyone* can be a divorce mediator, there being as yet no legal requirements for training or certification. But this should not be taken as an invitation to jump in. Mediation requires not only a great deal more skill than most persons have, but also a great deal of knowledge. Mediators must know what the laws are and what procedures must be followed, as well as knowing a great deal about marriage, and psychology in general. It is a demanding profession, loaded with possibilities for failure, and failure here can have lasting consequences.

As mediation is more and more taking the place of traditional litigation, there have arisen professional organizations that sponsor meetings and workshops. Sometimes training is also offered through universities. Many persons, untrained in legal practice, are moving into the profession, greatly enriching it.

In any case, when you seek out a mediator to help in your own situation, it is of the utmost importance to learn his or her own background and approach. Do not assume that there is some standard approach which all mediators share. How your mediator goes about things can make a vast difference as to what your future as a divorced person will be like.

If you think you want to battle, then do not look to mediation. Find a good lawyer, who is likely to turn out to be an expensive one. If, on the other hand, you want to avoid warfare, but are convinced that your partner does not, then you will perhaps do best with a mediator who uses the standard legalistic approach, discussed in the previous section.

But if you and your partner can both be reasonable, neither wishing to take advantage of the other, then you will both do best with a mediator who will be guided, not so much by the precedents established in legal practice, but by the desire to reach a result maximally acceptable to you both. This is what I call "open" mediation. The expression is my own, and will be meaningless to mediators, but you can easily identify it.

Mediation is likely to begin with an "intake." That is, one or both partners, finding themselves headed for divorce, will get in touch with a mediation center, very likely discovered through the telephone directory or from friends. This initial inquiry is likely to come from just one of the partners, who may be seriously distraught. Both partners will be urged to come for the initial interview, for which there will be an "intake fee," of perhaps fifty dollars, more or less, depending on the resources of the couple. This

session will help you learn what kind of mediator you are confronted with. This mediator may speak as if mediation is the same
everywhere, but in fact it is not.

Sometimes a couple will turn up for the initial interview so angry
that they do not want to speak to each other, and there are even examples of those who go through the entire mediation, not wanting even
to look at each other. Mediation can sometimes proceed to a more or
less acceptable conclusion under such circumstances, but the best
procedure, which I am calling "open" mediation, cannot.

By the second meeting, or possibly the third, the couple will
have drawn up a complete inventory of their assets—real estate,
investments, special collections, bank accounts, pension provisions, and so on, together with rough profiles of their children—
ages, gender, schools, anything that will be relevant to the discussion. Typically, the mediator, adopting an open approach, will now
have a foundation for getting things out in the open and providing
a general picture of whatever might be at issue.

Now the mediation begins, and proceeds in the manner
described. The primary function of the mediator will be to nourish
the atmosphere of cooperation, to discourage any spirit of competition for this or that valuable asset or, above all, the temptation of
either party to gain an advantage over the other or to try to control
things. There will not be a winner and a loser. Both should win. In
the nature of the case, neither will win everything he or she might
be entitled to or even want, but both should end up with what is
most important to them.

Under this procedure, then, the mediator does *not* simply do the
work of two attorneys. In fact, only one attorney needs to be
involved. The mediator uses his skills to get the two parties to agree
on everything at issue, writes up the agreement, they sign it, and it
is handed over to *one* attorney, who satisfies himself that it is in
proper form for submission to the court. This may require only the
most cursory examination, and very likely, even less close attention
by the judge, who will incorporate it in his divorce decree. When a

divorcing couple arrives at a settlement that is clearly acceptable to both, then a judge has no incentive to raise difficulties, even if, were he to study the agreement, it might appear to him that one of the two parties is getting the better of the deal. If neither party has any objection, then neither should the judge. To this it should be added, however, that if either party should at a later date feel taken advantage of, then he or she will have little sympathy from a judge, who will take the view that you agreed to this, so now live with it.

It is obvious that this open approach absolutely requires a great deal of cooperation. It will not work for a wrangling couple, or when either side seeks an advantage over the other, or when one of them, typically the husband, is of a controlling nature and the other accustomed to yielding to his way of doing things.

A difficulty with what I have called the "standard" mediation is that the mediator does, at some points, seem to make the decisions, simply by telling the partners what, in the light of what the law accepts, they *must* do. To use again our previous example, he might tell the husband that he *has* to share his pension with his wife, whether it seems reasonable or not. Standard mediation thus violates a basic principle of all mediation, in that the mediator does in fact make some of the decisions, whether or not this is justified. Open mediation, by contrast, while it cannot disregard divorce law, is not bound by it, so decisions can in fact be arrived at by the divorcing parties. The difference between the two approaches can be seen from our previous examples. The clearest scenario would be where retirement benefits are involved. A lawyer will insist that her client get her share of, say, the husband's benefits. Likewise, the "standard" mediator. In open mediation entitlements need not even be considered, if the two parties want to do things differently.

Thus, the mediator need not be entirely guided by the presuppositions of attorneys in resolving ownership of pension benefits. If, for example, the husband feels strongly that these were earned by him and therefore should remain with him, then the mediator can try to find something that the wife feels strongly about and seek a trade-off. For example, she may want, at considerable expense, to pursue professional training of some sort, and the husband can agree to that, even though he would not be obligated to by any precedents or customary models of law. Or suppose the wife wants to remain in the house they have shared, and to keep all the furniture there. An agreement might be arranged for this, with the understanding that she will pay off the mortgage.

Custody problems can sometimes be resolved by the same approach. Instead, for example, of assuming that the mother has some kind of prior claim to the children, the two might agree to share custody, under some arrangement that is not recognized in law. It might even be agreed that one or the other could have the children at any time that is not inconvenient for both, taking into account the children's needs and wishes. Even something that is that vague will be accepted by a court, provided both parents have agreed to it, but a lawyer, or standard mediator, might insist on something far more specific.

Other matters can be similarly treated. The wife might, for example, want to be kept as the beneficiary of any life insurance, even in the event that the husband might remarry. This could go into the agreement, even though, as an attorney would point out, it would be very difficult to enforce. The husband could at any point stop paying the premiums, for example, without notifying the wife. Nevertheless, the fact that something has been formally agreed to, and embodied in a decree, is a powerful force for compliance.

Such examples illustrate the enormous advantage of open mediation. What divorcing people actually need, and what they might be entitled to, can be very different. By concentrating on needs, rather than legal entitlements, it is very possible to arrive at an amicable settlement, and what is of great importance, civility and even friendship are made possible. Concentrating on entitlements, on the other hand, exacerbates resentments, and the two go their separate ways embittered by what they see as having been forced upon them. Everyone suffers—wife, husband, and children.

There are certain to be some requirements of law that cannot be met by this procedure. For example, there must be some specific ground for divorce, and the choice of grounds will be limited. Sometimes the choice will be easy—for example, if "irreconcilable differences" is allowable. But sometimes it will not be easy, as when the choice is, say, between adultery, or ongoing drunkenness, or physical abuse, or imprisonment. No one wants these hung on him, even as a groundless formality. If abandonment is a permissible ground, then this can usually be met by having a valid separation agreement. Such an agreement can be composed by the divorcing couple themselves, or by the mediator, and all it needs to say is that they agree to live separate and apart. The law may require that such separation last for one year or perhaps two years, but this does not mean that the couple must *in fact* live separate and apart; they can go on living together as before if physical separation would be impractical. No one will come around to check on this, and the court will accept the agreement, properly notarized to validate its dates, as sufficient proof of abandonment. A judge is entirely satisfied with a notarized and dated separation agreement; he doesn't care whether the parties were or were not living together during part or most of that time. Judges tend to be practical. My ex-wife and I had a separation agreement but continued living together for convenience. New York State requires a one-year separation. We had been living apart only four months. What mattered was the date on the separation agreement. Mediators know this.

Needless to say, a trained mediator will know what the special requirements of the law are and find some way of meeting them, or, at least, of appearing to meet them.

winning

The basic assumption underlying everything we have been saying is that you want to win, which means to get as much as possible of what you want, whether in marriage or, if it comes to that, in divorce. The other assumption is that you are capable of being rational, which means, in this case, that you *know* what you want. Many people—perhaps most—do not. They want to be happy, of course, but do not know how to get there. They are like the child who wants to eat the colorful pills he found in the medicine cabinet, or the drunk who desperately wants another drink, or the woman who wants to marry a millionaire.

In marriage, you wanted, and confidently expected, happiness. Did you get it? Maybe, but more likely, you did not. Perhaps it ended in divorce. Or perhaps you are married, maybe long married, but stuck with less than you hoped for. Or perhaps you can truly say you are happy, that is, not unhappy, but that happiness arises from sources other than your marriage, such as your work. This falls short of being the greatest happiness that life can offer, of being totally and indestructibly in love, and having that love returned for the rest of your days.

Many writers on marriage declare that this is not reality, that such love does not exist in marriage, that marriage is made up of compromises. You learn to get along. It is not uncommon, for example, for people, and even writers on the subject, to assume that all married people quarrel with fair regularity, that marriage is to some extent always a battle of wills, and that a successful marriage is therefore one in which partners can compromise, get along with each other, and keep things together.

Of course there is something to be said for this. Keeping some semblance of peace is better than constantly warring, if those are the alternatives, and sometimes imperfect marriages should be kept together for various reasons having nothing to do with happiness. But you do not need to settle for that. Peace, in marriage, should be the fruit of genuine love, not just the result of mutual restraint.

Consider marriage first. You wanted to find happiness there. Perhaps you thought that this would be achieved by marrying a woman of great beauty, or that it would follow upon worldly success that would open for both of you the sources of pleasure that are denied those of meager means—a beautiful house, or perhaps several, fine cars, nice things. Maybe you like to be in control and sought happiness by taking control of your partner. The eminent "eligible bachelor" is widely assumed to be very worth getting, for his social position, money, good looks, whatever. And so on— people's goals, in life and marriage, differ, and yet they are all the same in this: all are thought to be routes to happiness, which is the ultimate life goal of everyone. But some routes, instead of leading there, lead to the opposite. The high rate of divorce is proof of that.

Consider whether you are like the child who finds the inviting pills in the medicine chest. He gets what he wants—the pills—but he doesn't get what he wants when they turn out to be toxic. The drunk most surely wants another drink, but he didn't want to end up in the filth of the gutter, which is what he got. And the woman who managed to marry the millionaire, as she so desperately wanted, was not seeking the perhaps boring, perhaps controlling, perhaps abusive husband that this millionaire turned out to be.

But what of someone who passes up the specious allures and ends up loving her husband the rest of her life, and being totally loved in return? Here, there is no mistake. She really *does* get what she wants, which is the happiness that the others sought but missed. This is the lesson that anyone approaching divorce must have in mind, which is, knowing what you *really* want, and most of all, knowing how to get it. What you really want is to get on with your life, with the fulfillments that life still has to offer, and with the minimum of disruption. Whatever leads in the opposite direction, that is, to bitterness, frustration, and the loss of things that are truly dear to you, such as friendships and self-esteem, are things you do *not* want, however tempting they may be.

A lawyer is apt to think that you want "all you can get" even at the expense of your partner. He is mistaken, and so are you if you think that, too. And you may be so angry that what you want, that is, think you want, is revenge, the utter destruction of your partner, in return for what he has done to you. But things like this, you have to remind yourself, are not ends for their own sakes; they are the means to other things, and what they are most likely to lead to are not the conditions for finding a fulfilling life. You are, once again, like the child, lured by the colorful, tempting, but toxic pills.

Consider the following account:

> After my wife moved out and had, we thought, taken everything she thought she would need in the way of furniture and so on, she kept returning, to pick up some odd or end, and these became increasingly trivial. After she had taken her books, I started to find mine disappearing, one or two or a few at a time, books on things she had no interest in. Evidently she had decided they might bring a few dollars in a yard sale or something. Then went a cheap waste basket, and a tray, and a house thermometer. Finally, when she had removed some sheets of plywood from the barn, which were worth very little and absolutely nothing to her, I asked her to stop, and she did. A few weeks later she asked me to come and get the plywood.

What was going on here, obviously, is that the wife had gotten way beyond consideration of what she needed to get on with her life. She had already reached that point, and beyond. The small items that were disappearing could easily have been purchased. But she was now thinking just in terms of what might have some value, however small. There it was, for the taking. Seeing the plywood in her garage must have been a reminder that she had stooped to pettiness.

By getting caught up in the need to win everything, you risk becoming your own enemy. There is, for example, a case of a woman who got deeply involved in the question of who would get the cans of paint in the basement. She finally agreed to let her husband have the opened ones and she would have the full ones. Needless the say, her lawyer billed her for the considerable time it took to arrive at this solution. These are but glaring examples of wanting something, but not, in fact, knowing what you want.

The very first step, then, in dissolving a marriage, hopefully by mediation, is to have clearly in mind what, ultimately, you want. This can always be described as what is needed for getting on with your life and finding such fulfillment as life still has to offer, nothing else. Anything that does not contribute to that is something you neither need nor want, even if it is, like the pills the child finds, tempting. The consequences of looking at things this way may seem to be of little significance, but in fact, they are enormous, as we shall see.

guidelines

Mediation is not for everyone. It would be if people were all rational, but reason is usually the first thing to go when a marriage begins to come apart. Faced with possible insecurity and the threat to one's self-esteem, people revert to childhood, and soon not only reason but even basic civility disappear. Even clergypersons have noted how rapidly everything disintegrates once a marriage begins to dissolve.

It is overwhelmingly important to control these negative emotions and at least cultivate civility, for this is the only way you can win. Mediation, where the partners allow it to work, is vastly better than litigation, just in terms of cost and time, but more important, it can enable both parties to win in every way that counts, or at least not to lose. In drawn out litigation, it cannot be sufficiently stressed, both parties lose, and when it leads to bitter resentment, the loss is very great, both to the couple and to any children they may have. Moreover, if one of the parties resorts to battle, even to subtle battle carried on only in words, and the other cultivates an unwavering civility, then it is the latter who comes out ahead under the guidance of a skillful mediator. Pacifism must be the rule in divorce, and if the other side cannot control fear and resentment, then it is your side that is almost certain to be the one that survives intact. Once you have foregone warfare and turned to mediation to resolve things, you must steadfastly cultivate a certain attitude and demeanor. Your impulse will be to do the very opposite, but that is a recipe for defeat.

Here, then, are some guidelines. Most of them would flow automatically from heeding what was said earlier about the sense of self-worth that governs all human behavior, for that is the first thing that one feels imperiled by a divorce situation. *Any* dispute threatens it, for the circumstances raise the specter of being the *loser*. Faced with this, your impulse is to fight back. And it can not be too often repeated that this is a formula for losing. Why, for example, are divorcing couples so often reduced to dickering over insignificant things? It is not because of what is at stake, but just because neither wants to be the one to give in, to be cast in the role of the loser.

Rule one: Do not say anything, or bring up any consideration, that the other can interpret as casting doubt on his or her worth as a person. For example, do not allow even the most casual comment to slip from your lips that could have this effect, such as "Well, it would be just like her to . . ." or "That's what he always did whenever the kids were involved," or "She never seemed willing to . . ." It makes not the slightest difference if such a comment might be incontestably *true*. The effect is to make the other defensive.

If, for example, the husband was, in fact, an indulgent parent, do not say, "He always just let the kids do whatever they wanted." That just invites an attempt at rebuttal, and nothing has moved forward. Say instead, "I tended to be rather strict with the children, maybe too strict, but I sometimes felt that maybe he went a little too far the other way." This makes exactly the same point, but removes the inclination of the other to even things up by saying, for example, "She just wants to blame me for the kids' behavior when it was really her need to control that caused the problem." There is no way of moving things along when this sort of thing goes on.

Again, do not allow yourself to say, "She just spent money like there was no tomorrow." Try instead, "My family never had much, and this may have made me excessively frugal, but I did sometimes feel that we might have controlled expenses a little better." The first invites the response "He just wanted us to live like paupers," while the second, it should be noted, says "we," not "he."

One more example: Do not say, "He wanted to spend all his time with his pals, when we could have been doing things together." Instead, "Maybe I'm excessively needy, but there were times when he was with his friends and I did miss him terribly." That, again, says the same thing, but has the opposite, desired effect. It is totally disarming.

I have dwelt on this, perhaps overlong, because, however simple the point may seem, it is probably the hardest thing for people to do. And this is not being urged simply out of an abstract respect for politeness, but because it is the first step toward getting what you want. Your purpose is not just to look good, however deeply you may wish to, but rather, to get what you are after. Any satisfaction you might get by demeaning the other, however subtly or slightly, will be short-lived indeed. But what you get in your divorce settlement will be forever. Do what you can to ensure that it will be what you want, starting with this.

Rule two: Once you have both agreed to a cooperative approach and found a mediator seeking the same approach, do not try to take advantage of your partner's trust and cooperation to gain an advantage. Do not, for example, consult secretly with an attorney to plan strategy. The lawyer will want to point out certain tactics you might be able to pull off at an opportune time, or offer a strategy for "winning." He might also be able to call attention to certain weaknesses in the other's situation, or, perhaps, certain strengths that the other may be unaware of—things to beware of, in other words.

Needless to say, such an approach would be totally out of keeping with the kind of mediation you have agreed to, and would doom it to failure. If your impulse is to "win," in the sense of delivering defeat to your partner and gaining a "victory" for yourself, then you have chosen the wrong kind of mediation. Be open, so that you can *both* seek the aid of lawyers, and either let them carry on the battle, or else go to a mediator who approves of this way of doing things. You will then get what you are in some sense entitled to, but no one will really win with respect to the things that are important.

Rule three: Do not cast blame. A spouse might say, "Well, he's the one who's destroyed this marriage, by getting involved with that woman and then lying to me all the time." This may be completely true, but what is the point in bringing it up when he, and presumably the mediator, already know it? Why rub it in, other than to give yourself a sense of victimhood? If you were litigating the breakup, then your attorney would indeed seize upon that behavior to score a point against the other attorney, but that is precisely what you are trying to avoid by mediation. Do not make yourself your own victim.

Rule four: Maintain the status quo of finances. Do not, for example, cancel credit cards in both your names or joint checking accounts in order to foreclose her cleaning them out. This would be interpreted as a clear threat, certain to produce countermeasures of some sort. Instead, make it perfectly clear that you will *not* do that, encourage her to put charges on the cards and write checks in the same way she always has, and indicate, preferably in the presence of the mediator, that you trust her not to take advantage of this. People always respond better to trust than to threat, simply because violating a clear trust amounts to violating one's own sense of decency and self-worth.

A powerful retiring chief executive officer of a huge corporation, seeing that his marriage was rapidly crumbling, canceled all joint accounts, reestablishing them in his name only. It was perhaps the biggest blunder of his lifetime, for his wife then made publicly known his enormous assets, together with all the outrageous benefits his board of directors had bestowed on him, involving multiple luxury homes, use of company jet planes, and so on. This information resulted in such public outcry that the directors felt compelled to press him to cancel most of those huge benefits and privileges. He had imagined that he could call all the shots with respect to his wife, just as he had been accustomed to doing with his business subordinates.

Do not make this kind of mistake. The risk to your assets, while not zero, is slight if you keep the status quo and a policy of trust, whereas it is greatly magnified by overt distrust.

Rule five: Do not take hard stands. To take a hard stand, that is, to declare in advance that you are going to insist on this or that, will not only result in similar hard stands on the other side, but will give that side a strong incentive to undermine you. You will be seen as stubborn and irrational. This does not mean that you cannot have in mind some basic positions that you are intent on, but you will be much more likely to get them if you do not declare that you are going to, no matter what.

For example, you may feel strongly that your children shall be brought up in your religion, which is not shared by your husband. Do not insist on this before the matter has even come up. Instead, seek an opening to introduce it, perhaps an opening created by the mediator, and preferably accompanied by some concession on your part. Suppose your husband wants very strongly to have the children during certain vacations, and let us suppose you have no very strong objection to that. Yield on that point, with the understanding that he will have no objection to your wishes respecting religion. It will thus appear as voluntary give and take, even though you have given nothing that matters much to you.

The same can apply to larger matters, such as the kind of support you will need. Suppose, for example, you can increase your job opportunities by certain training that is perhaps expensive. With the right approach, your husband might easily agree to this, the more so if it is made to look like generosity on his part rather than something that is wrung from him.

Rule six: Listen. Try to understand what is important to your wife, even if you are most reluctant to provide it. You need not agree to what you hear, but keep your disagreements to yourself as long as you can, and then raise the difficulty in another context— such as, your reasonable needs. To try to silence or squelch your partner in advance, with a refusal even to consider what is being said, will set things back for you even more than for her, because you will appear unreasonable, not only to her but to the mediator, whose help you are seeking. But again, this does not mean that you have to simply give in to demands, but only, that you have to listen to them, with patience.

Rule seven: Do not try to bludgeon with some hitherto unsuspected weapon, even though it may seem to you to be a powerful one. Suppose, for example, your husband has a valuable collection of some sort, rare books perhaps, important to him but of no real interest to you. It has simply never occurred to him that these might not be kept intact and in his possession. You, however, have learned that, since they were purchased during the marriage, you have a claim on them, too, and that he could be ordered to sell them and split the proceeds. Don't drop that bomb. What you are seeking is cooperation, leading to results agreeable to you both. You are not looking for weapons. That will only lead him to find counter weapons.

Rule eight: Do not wax sanctimonious. "I take seriously the vows we both made at our wedding." This, of course, implies that he does *not* take them seriously, and is therefore a lesser person than you. That gains nothing. No marriage was ever held together by vows. To invoke them at this point is hypocrisy, and will be seen as such by any intelligent mediator.

Rule nine: Do not think in terms of entitlement. This overlaps our rule seven. Of course, you have certain obvious entitlements— with respect to your children, for example—but try to get beyond this way of thinking, and concentrate instead on what can be cooperatively arrived at, even, perhaps, at the expense of some entitlements, such as pension benefits. What is important is what you both *need*, not what you can count on getting.

Rule ten: Do not alienate the children. Do not even be tempted to bad-mouth your partner to the children, thinking you might, by weakening their respect and affection for him, strengthen your own hold on them. This rule must be scrupulously kept even if he is, in fact, not a good person. What the children see is a father. They do not want to think of him, their own father, as in any sense bad.

This rule is regularly urged by counselors, just in the light of the harm done to children by disregarding it. They need both parents, and in time, as they mature, they will see for themselves any limitations of character that either has. Even if the other person is a perfectly horrid person, perhaps a criminal, this should never be conveyed to the children by the other parent. Children see through everything sooner or later, and need no confirmation or disconfirmation of what they come to see. The only correct position by the "good" parent is either silence, or magnanimity. What is not sufficiently emphasized is that disparaging the other parent is a fairly good prescription for alienating the children from yourself, which is the very opposite of what you were seeking. For however much they may accept your disparagement now, the time will come when they will see things in a different light, which can result in acute resentment of you.

Rule eleven: Do not exhibit anger in the presence of the children. For parents to quarrel in front of children is unpardonable, even in a marriage that is not threatened by divorce. A divorcing couple raising their voices in front of their children releases in them an intense sense of insecurity. It will also, even many years later, impact negatively on their own marriages. Children grow up and enter marriage guided by the model of their parents, without reflecting on it, just as they absorb the language and accents of their parents.

This rule is violated with such regularity that some judges have found it necessary to arrange transfers of children, for visitations, through a third person, so that the parents need not even lay eyes on each other. Furthermore, it is obvious that such behavior renders mediation totally impossible. If adult people cannot restrain themselves even in the presence of their children, then what possibility is there of civility and cooperation in the presence of a mediator?

It is all too common, but totally unnecessary, for divorcing couples to behave like children. It would be bad enough in itself if it did not virtually guarantee that both will lose the very things that they are trying to win.

Rule twelve: Never raise a barrier to communication. A happily married couple can often go a long time with minimal communication. They don't need to talk, for they virtually read each other's minds. Understanding is automatic. But a divorcing couple must not maintain silence, nor can they settle for communication through a third person. If the third person is a mediator, then his role is to facilitate direct communication between the two parties, not to act as the medium of it. Avoid, then, such declarations as "That's all I have to say on the matter," or "This is not open to discussion." And never, if the discussion is by telephone, hang up on the other.

None of this means, of course, that you have to *accept* whatever is being said. It means only that nothing, however outrageous, is to be rejected out-of-hand. If the other side is, or seems, unreasonable, then it is precisely the role of a mediator to help see things in a clearer light, and this, of course, may require both parties to get a better understanding of the other side. This is clearly impossible if that other side cannot even be heard.

Of course, rules like these could be spun out without end, but this sampling is sufficient to enable you to understand the spirit in which mediation must proceed. Bear in mind always that a good mediator does not solve problems *for* you. *You and your partner have to find the solutions yourselves.* The mediator simply, and literally, *mediates* between you; that is, helps *you* find your solutions. Success in this depends not only on the mediator's skills, but on *your* willingness to cooperate. Solutions will not be found unless you are willing to give the same thought and consideration to the needs of the other party that you give to your own. That way, you will win, precisely because you will *both* win. A win for one side does not mean loss for the other. If that were your goal, namely, *defeat* for the other, then you would find a good lawyer, pay him dearly—and take your chances.

magnanimity

The perfect way to deal with marital breakup is with magnanimity. Because of the inherent limitations of human nature, it is, however, something that very few are capable of. Magnanimity means, literally, "greatness of soul." It was an ideal deeply prized by the wisest philosophers of antiquity. It is not easily defined, but it can be illustrated as follows.

When Robert E. Lee surrendered to General Grant to end the Civil War, he had every reason to assume that he would be hanged for treason. Such had become standard practice among modern victors in war. Instead, General Grant received him with an open hand, and the two spent the time reminiscing about the past they had shared, their officers meanwhile retiring to have dinner together. The same spirit is contained in Lincoln's famed address at Gettysburg, in which, in opposition to the policies of vindictiveness then advocated by powerful forces, he set forth the policy of malice toward none and charity for all.

How can such an attitude possibly apply to marital dissolution? It almost never does, of course. Partners in breakup have little but disdain for each other, become at best strangers, and at worse implacable enemies. Probably no other relationship provides such fertile ground for bitterness. Here we have two people who have loved and trusted each other, and now both feel not only betrayed, but profoundly threatened in their most vital interests, even basic self-respect. It is needless to say that these feelings produce nothing that is good. On the contrary, they threaten all the things that matter. Wars are never won. This has been the underlying theme of this book.

Civility is sometimes possible, especially in partners who are well-educated, without children, and without large holdings. These individuals can sometimes, without assigning blame, agree that their marriage is not working, go their separate ways, and even remain, at least on the surface, friends.

But what, short of reaching for every weapon you have, can you do when you feel deeply threatened, knowing that your partner has a resourceful attorney who has no regard at all for the things that matter to you, who will take advantage of any opening he can to win at your expense, so that you are confronted with the possibility of losing your children, and even your basic security? Paranoia sets in, and, worst of all, you become your *own* enemy, setting yourself up for defeat. Attack simply produces counterattack, and when divorce becomes a kind of tug of war, neither side is overcome. Both lose.

No matter how odious your partner's behavior, no matter how calculating and resourceful the attorney hired to do battle with you, your best course is always silence, at the very least, and what is known as stonewalling. Never respond in kind. Your partner can be reminded that weapons are available to you, too, but do not threaten to use them. Of course there may arise demands that you cannot ignore, such as an enforceable order to produce tax returns or what-ever, but your response can always be minimal and not accompa-nied with counteraction or threat of action. Avoid, by all means, wrangling, or even heated discussion. If accused, say nothing. Angry telephone calls can be treated with silence.

But what of magnanimity? This is something that goes well *beyond* withdrawal and silence, and yet, it can turn out to be your greatest strength. To be magnanimous is to respond to threat with positive friendliness, to speak well of whomever is speaking ill of you. It is, in the terms of scripture, not only to turn the other cheek, but to actually go the extra mile—to do *more* than expected. This may *look* like capitulation, but it is not. What finally matters in a divorce action is what is actually written in a court decree. Your very best possibility is to have a hand in that, and the best opportu-nity for that is to refrain totally from threat or battle, sustain com-munication, and thus blunt in advance every weapon that can be drawn against you.

Examples of magnanimity are, of course, not easy to find, because magnanimity in divorce is so exceedingly rare that it is generally considered beyond human capacity. Here, however, are four such examples:

> I learned that my wife was deeply involved with her hairdresser, and had been for some time, only recently discovered by me. I was devastated, and found it hard to believe that she could be more strongly drawn to him than to me. He was a man of reasonably good looks and much charm, but otherwise of little significance. I felt utterly betrayed and wanted to cover my hurt with outrage, and to reach for the most insulting of epithets to heap not only on him, but on her, but something restrained me. She was quite aware that I knew what was going on, but I managed not to bring it up. I said nothing, but went on with life as best I could. Then to this I added outward expressions of friendliness, even noting, at one point, that it was no wonder that she should attract another man, given her good looks. Her reaction to that was stunned amazement. Not much was said over the next few weeks, and I think we were both pretty miserable. Then she learned that this other man had been badly and maybe fatally injured on his motorcycle and was in the hospital. This news produced cold silence between us. My own feelings about it were ambivalent. But then I found myself asking her, "Would you like to be alone?" She didn't know how to respond. The other guy survived the accident, but she never took up with him again. Instead, she returned to me, and while the pain of it all never left me, the marriage survived.

It takes very little understanding of human nature to infer how all that would have turned out had this husband chosen to do battle—a war which, from the standpoint of divorce law, he would easily have won. But the marriage would have been destroyed, buried in bitterness.

And here is the second example:

> We had arrived at an acceptable settlement, all incorporated in our divorce decree, but little problems and frictions nevertheless arose from time to time, mostly having to do with the children.

During one somewhat tense encounter, when I could feel my former wife's unspoken hostility, I found myself saying to her, "Any request you ever make, having to do with either money or the children, the answer will always be 'yes.'" I think that moment marked a turning point in our relationship. She never again did or said anything that led me to feel the least bit threatened, and she had seen clearly that I was not going to threaten her. We have remained friends, of sorts, ever since, and our mode of interacting has been unwavering cooperation. She has never made any unreasonable request having to do with either the children or money, and we have both, as a matter of policy, happily taken each other's needs into account with respect to paying for things for the children and arranging which parent they should be with. If for any reason I want to do something with them, she readily agrees, and I do exactly the same. It works out very well for both of us, and, for the children.

Our third example is reconstructed from a thirdhand report:

I knew the man my wife had left me for and, although I didn't know him very well, he seemed like a very nice guy, the kind I would probably like if I knew him better—that is, until he broke up my marriage. It wasn't a very good marriage, but still, it was a marriage. One evening I encountered them both in a theater lobby. My impulse was to walk away, but somehow I didn't. I guess I thought it would look like weakness. Then I found myself shaking hands with him, and said, "You have a wonderful woman there. Take good care of her!" He was speechless, and I think I was almost as surprised myself.

And finally:

How was I going to feel about my husband's former wife, the mother of their three children?

And how, I wondered, would they feel about me?

Would she feel comfortable leaving the children with me

sometimes? I knew that even small children pick up animosities even when they are mostly unspoken. She's a nice person, and I liked her from the first time we met. I hoped she'd feel the same way about me.

She settled things when, early on, when all six of us—three adults and three children—were having dinner together, she told me, "I hope my daughter grows up to be just like you." I was flabbergasted! I almost cried.

Soon afterward my friends were astonished to learn that all six of us would be vacationing together. I had to admit that it was a little unusual, but we felt it was better for the kids to have one extended vacation instead of breaking it up into two. Sometimes things were a little uncomfortable, but we worked things out. My husband listens to my concerns, and respects my feelings. And fortunately, his relationship with the mother of his children is much better than when they struggled with an unhappy marriage.

Now when one of the children comes up, gives me a big hug, and says, "I love you," I know that we have done things right.

In this last account we find magnanimity at its very best, displayed in all three of the adults involved. Not only were the children left unscarred, but the grown-ups as well. Everybody won.

It is worth reflecting, with respect to all these accounts, on what the effect would have been had these four given in to their perfectly natural and expected feelings of resentment, and exhibited these in their speech and behavior. That would have been easy, and destructive of the interests of everyone. The magnanimity they displayed, on the other hand, was totally disarming. It is quite impossible to attack, even in speech, someone who displays nothing but good feelings toward you, but who, in fact, could be expected to do the very opposite. Conflict never succeeds. And love never fails.

FIFTH LEVEL: SELF-MANAGED DIVORCE

What if there were a way of dissolving your marriage without turning to any lawyers, or even to a mediator, or any third person? What if you could write *your own terms*, thereby getting pretty much what you want and then getting on with your life with the minimum of friction and dislocation?

Actually, there is, but you will not find it described in any of the standard literature on mediation and divorce. It can be done, because it in fact is done, albeit rarely.

But just as mediation is not for everyone, neither is this. Mediation does not work for couples whose self-interest is clouded by the desire to win in what amounts to a battle. Similarly the procedure about to be described is not for everyone, for it requires you to go one step *beyond* civility and cooperation. It requires you to be rational to a degree that few people can rise to. It requires you to be magnanimous. For what it requires is that you put your spouse's needs *ahead* of your own. This, of course, sounds like a recipe for losing, but in fact, for those few who are up to it, it is a guarantee that you will win—not win through victory over an adversary, or even through compromise, but win exactly what you want.

This approach, moreover, not only saves time and money, even over mediation, but it ensures ongoing cooperation between the divorcing parties. Needing a name for this, let us call it "self-managed divorce." Here is an example from real life:

> We had been married for twelve years, and had two children, when my wife began to be restless and increasingly distant. She had left college her senior year to get married and had begun to regret it. Finally, she said that she wanted to leave, become completely independent and find some way to prepare herself for a teaching career. I was completely devastated by this, for until then, it had been a totally joyous marriage, for her as well as for me. Until then, I could not imagine that the marriage could fail.
>
> My first reaction was to find ways to make it impossible for

her to go, and find inducements for her to stay. She had no resources whatever, and certainly no ground for divorce. I reminded her of the promises she had made. My threats became less and less subtle. All this only created resentment, and it finally became clear that nothing was going to make her stay. So I decided to fight back, since it was clear to me that I had all the cards, and she had nothing to fight with. But then she reminded me that there were still ways she could hurt me, even if she were the loser.

Finally, I had a novel idea. I realized that I could not hurt her, because she meant so much to me, and was also the mother of my children, so I resolved to at least try somehow to retain her friendship and respect. One day I asked her to decide just what she might need in order to fulfill her desire to be independent and establish herself in a teaching career, to think about it, then write it down. And I did the same; not indicating what I wanted, which was, to have her stay, because that was impossible, and not saying what I thought I could successfully demand, because that would truly threaten her, but what I thought I would need, just as I had asked her to do.

She indicated that she would need a place to live and the means to finish her education and get a teaching certificate, toward which she would be able to contribute nothing at all.

I said that I would need to stay in our house, keep my considerable retirement benefits for myself, and have the children with me whenever I wanted them.

Amazingly, I realized that I could meet her needs, completely, though at great cost, and she said she could meet mine.

Then we discussed the details: how much support would she need, and for how long, plus such matters as life insurance, cars, house furnishings, ownership of the house, and so on. Having limited ourselves to actual needs on the large issues, we easily agreed on the details, with only minimal discussion.

Then I put all that in an agreement. Neither of us had consulted any lawyer, or even any mediator, but a lawyer friend suggested the format for such an agreement. He did not know, or even suggest any of its contents.

Then we took the agreement to a lawyer, whom my wife knew but I had never met, told her we didn't want any advice concerning its contents, but only to have it incorporated in a divorce decree.

Meanwhile, I became quite caught up in the house search, and finally, as agreed, bought one for her, only a few miles away, the title in her name. The credit cards and checking account were kept in joint name, and she used them for all her educational costs. She never used them for any other purchases. I stayed in our house; the title to it was transferred to me, and all the furniture I needed was left there. No disputes arose over this. And no claims were made on my retirement benefits.

The divorce decree finally came, signed by a judge I had never heard of. The total cost of this was three hundred dollars, which we shared.

Looking back, I realize that I gave up a lot more than I had to. In that sense I was clearly the loser. She gave up nothing. But the important thing is that we remained friends, or at least, not foes. She has never uttered a word against me, nor I against her. Neither of us claimed custody of the children, and we worked out informal arrangements that suit us both. The children are completely undamaged by this, having never heard a word in anger or even less than the total respect we have for each other. She became very successful in her work, eventually earning more than I ever had, and is happy to share the costs of raising the children. I certainly could have arranged things better with respect to buying her the house we found, which ate up most of my savings, but we both did, in fact, get everything we needed. All that was ten years ago, and meanwhile, after a period of deep loneliness, I remarried, and found an even better life than before.

Obviously, that is the best possible way to dissolve a marriage. All it requires is that both partners forego not only battle, but even competition, thinking first of each other. Everyone gets what he needs and, in this case, as it turned out, everything that each really wanted. The standard advice, that to win in divorce you need a good lawyer, a good bank account, and a good psychiatrist, is not realism. It is foolishness.

Here then, in some detail, is how to manage your own divorce. First, you agree with your spouse that neither of you will seek advice from any attorney and, for the time being, you also agree not to seek the assistance of any mediator. You are, instead, going to try to do everything yourself. That way, the two of you will be in complete control.

Step one: Your first step will be a *separation agreement.* This is nothing more than a written agreement, of a fairly informal nature, signed by both of you and your signatures *authenticated by a notary public.* The purpose of the latter is not to ensure the validity of the signatures, but rather, to establish the *date* of the agreement. This will prove to be important later on.

In many states separation for a stated amount of time—typically a year for some states, two years for others—is considered to be, by itself, a valid ground for divorce, without any implication of fault. Eventually, when divorce papers are actually submitted to a court for approval, one party or the other may allege "abandonment," but this need not carry any implication of blame. It will simply be a technicality, the term used by the "plaintiff" as the reason for dissolving the marriage, the "plaintiff" being the one who remained or will remain in the house that the two had hitherto shared.

But here the important point must be made that this agreement does not, contrary to appearance, require that you and your spouse actually separate. This is often difficult to do, simply because it would be a great dislocation and cost too much. The two of you can go right on sharing the same roof. No one is going to come around to check on whether you are or are not still living together. Objections *could* be raised, but since there are no lawyers involved, no one would have any reason to make an issue of it. The existence of the agreement, with date validated by a notary, will in virtually every jurisdiction be considered ample proof of separation.

Such an agreement also enables you to file income tax returns on the same basis that divorced people can. For example, you need not file joint returns—*but you may*, since you are still married. More significantly, if support payments ("alimony") are made to either party, in accordance with terms actually embodied in your separation agreement, then these can be deducted from the tax liability even though you are not actually divorced. This can amount to a very considerable savings, since alimony is deducted from gross income, not taxable income.

As for the agreement itself, it needs only to be clear what is being said and agreed to. Thus, it can follow some such format as this:

An Agreement

Between John Doe and Mary Smith Doe, husband and wife, concerning the conditions of their separation.

Contemplating the dissolution of our marriage, we agree henceforth to live separate and apart, and we further agree to the following terms of separation:

1. SUPPORT: Here you specify what payments will be made by which party for ongoing support of the other ("alimony"), when and how they will be made, and so on.
2. CHILDREN: Here you spell out how the children's expenses will be paid and by whom, who the children will live with, the conditions, dates, or whatnot for the children to be shared, and so on. Exactitude is not needed here; simply an indication that the children's needs, and those of the parents with respect to them, will be met.
3. MISCELLANEOUS: Here you spell out any other matters of possible importance to either of you, such as who will have use of the car or cars, what, if anything, will be done with credit cards and other joint accounts, any unusual expenses, such as medical costs, use of personal possessions, and so on.

It is that simple. Such a separation agreement might not require more than a single page. While it will technically amount to a legal contract, it should not be viewed in that light at all. What it amounts to is an *understanding* between two people, willing to cooperate, and its legal significance will arise later, if and when you decide upon actual divorce.

Step two: The second step is a transition. It is needless to say that no couple would consider separation and enter into the rudimentary formality of a written separation agreement if they did not perceive that their marriage does not seem to be working. Still, a separation is not a divorce. During this time various possibilities arise. You might, for example, continue living together, simply out of convenience, or perhaps even because one or both hope to put things back together. Or you may really separate, to live apart, going your separate ways. What your respective relationships with others will be during that transition is up to you. *Neither should make any demands on the other*, with respect to extramarital involvements or whatever. You are not divorced, but *neither are you married* in any real sense, whatever may be the legalities. So the separation might, and most likely will, result in the complete breakdown of the marriage, or it might, instead, become a period of healing, enabling you to restore the marriage after all.

Whatever happens, it is of the utmost importance that the spirit of mutual respect and cooperation continue. This is absolutely vital if the next stage is to be possible, namely, a final, unmediated settlement, to be incorporated in a divorce decree, arrived at solely by the couple themselves without the interference of any attorneys and possibly without even the assistance of a mediator. The only necessary involvement of an attorney will be the filing of the final agreement with the court.

Step three: This step is the hardest, because instead of entering into a contest, by litigation, or into a series of trade-offs, by mediation, you have to each try to think first of the needs of your partner.

When a divorce is litigated, the final terms and conditions, having to do with support payments, custody, visitation rights, division of property, and so on, are drawn up by lawyers, in consultation with their clients and with each other. This document, which becomes part of the divorce decree rendered by a court of law, is thus the result of a contest, often painfully arrived at and burdensome to the losing party.

When a divorce settlement is mediated, then, ideally, it is the product of compromise, but, if all goes as it should, the terms are arrived at cooperatively, so that neither party needs to be the loser.

If you manage your own divorce settlement, however, your approach is different from both of these. Instead of each partner trying to get everything he or she can get, or everything he or she is entitled to, or even everything that he or she wants, you *reverse* this; that is, in a self-managed divorce, *you put the needs of your partner first, rather than your own needs*. This may at first strike one as an absurdity, even as a formula for losing, but once understood, you can see that it is quite the opposite.

Here is what you do. You ask your partner to think carefully about, and then write down, what he (or she) thinks he needs to *get on with his life*, with as little disruption as possible, and you do the same.

Notice the emphasis. Neither of you is thinking of what you might be able to *get*, or even what you *want*, considered out of the context of your overall life and interests. Instead, you are to visualize the kind of life you are accustomed to, your overall goals, the basic things that are important to your life, and then come up with some idea of what you might need in order to get on with that life, as thus envisioned. Thus, having asked your partner to do this, objectively and in the spirit of cooperation, you do the same.

Next—and this is the important part—you each try to determine what you can do to meet the needs *of the other*, as thus set forth. It is not presumed here that each of you will be able to meet all the needs of the other, but then again, *you might*, and it is very likely that you will be able to go a long way toward that end. And it is, of course, still assumed that you will, both of you, set forth only what you think you might actually need, and not, what you think you are entitled to, or what would be "fair," or even what you want out of the settlement. Your thinking has to be entirely in the context of a basic life, as actually and realistically envisioned.

If you can manage this basic step—and, to be sure, relatively few people would be able to do this, human nature being what it is—then, as you can see, you *both* win in the only way that really matters. No one turns out to be the loser, even if, from a legalistic standpoint, one or the other may end up giving more than he or she has to. That simply does not matter.

For example, suppose the wife, having thought carefully about her life and how, realistically, she would like to have it go henceforth, comes up with something like the following:

She decides that she would like to remain in the house they have occupied together, with the mortgage paid up, keeping the children there and in the same school district. Further, she would like to become a nurse, and to that end would need to have the cost of such training, together with living expenses while in training, paid, after which she would need no further support. She would also need a car, life insurance protection for herself and the children until they are out of college, and health insurance coverage for herself and the children until she could obtain it through a future employer.

Her husband, meanwhile, guided by the same considerations of actual needs, comes up with the following:

He hopes sooner or later to remarry. He would like to have the wherewithal to buy another house. It is of great importance to him that he keep a close relationship with the children, which would mean having them with him for considerable periods. He also wants to be sure that all retirement benefits that have been set aside by his employer will go entirely to him. And he wants an assurance that, if he should lose most or all of his income for any reason, then any support payments would be adjusted accordingly.

Now, having arrived at that stage, and written out what they each think they would need to get on with their lives, they exchange what they have written, to see how far they can go *in meeting each other's needs*. They find, perhaps, that it might be possible to meet them all, in which case, they both will have won.

Of course, some details need to be worked out now: amount and duration of support payments, what to do about unanticipated expenses on either side, how to deal with any serious illness, and so on. Perhaps there will need to be some compromise, but, perhaps not.

If this self-managed agreement has worked so far, then all that remains is to put it in writing, which will be the final step. But if, on the other hand, it does *not* work—if either side finds it impossible to meet the needs of the other—then they can turn to mediation. Even so, mediation will now be vastly easier, for both have a fairly clear idea of what they need, and have already established a spirit of cooperation.

What needs to be stressed at this point is that, approached in this way, each is likely to find that he or she has expressed a willingness to forego advantages that they actually had, but what they have gained is more important. Both spouses can get on with the life they want for themselves, within the realm of possibility. Neither is the loser. Both win—not by going all out to get all they can for themselves, but rather, all they can for each other.

And notice what each has, in a sense, given up. The wife could, for example, demand custody of the children, with a good chance of getting it, but at the cost of great resentment on the part of their father. Or she could claim her share of the pension benefits when the time comes, since she earned them as much as he did, by taking care of the house and the children while he was away working. But she doesn't really need them. And she could insist on sharing any increases in income that he might receive in the future. Indeed, no law can compel her to gain an income for herself, whether through nursing or anything else, so she could demand support payments for life. But again, in the light of her plans, she does not need them.

The husband, on the other hand, need not yield so readily on the house, since he has lived there, too, and, perhaps, has even been responsible for all the payments to date. An attorney might readily ask, Why do you want to give her all that? And what if she should sell the house? Should all the proceeds go to her? These are questions that are *not even relevant* to what the two are trying to achieve by their approach. The object is not to get what you can, but to get what you need, precisely by seeing that, to the extent possible, the other gets what he or she needs.

Step four: Now the time has come to draw up the actual agreement. This will take time and care, and very likely require the help of a mediator. The main requirement is that it must be clear and readable.

The following, for example, could serve as a model.

An Agreement

Between John Doe and Mary Smith Doe, husband and wife, pertaining to the conditions of their separation and the dissolution of their marriage.

WE AFFIRM THAT:

    A. We were married in (city) on (date)

    B. We have four children by this marriage: (Names and birth dates).

CONDITIONS OF SEPARATION:

We agree to live henceforth separate and apart, and we further agree to the following conditions of separation.

    1. PRIVACY:

        We each agree to respect the independence and privacy of the other by not appearing unexpectedly at the residence of the other or querying anyone concerning comings and goings and associations.

2. CHILDREN:

(Here state custodial arrangements. These need not be very specific or precise; for example, you may want to *share* custody, working out living arrangements as time and circumstances permit, or you may want to be more specific such as summers with father, or whatever. If either wants assurance that the children will not be moved to a distant place or other jurisdiction, specify that they will not be removed from their present school district except by mutual consent. If religion is an issue, express what you agree to here.)

3. CHILD SUPPORT:

(Who is going to pay for what, for how long, or under what conditions, necessary medical costs, camp, and so on; who will pay college expenses; which, if any expenses are to be shared; what is to be done in case either parent gains, or loses, income; what life insurance and health benefit will be provided and by whom; and so on.)

4. SPOUSAL SUPPORT:

(What payments are to be made to which partner, and for how long, and under what conditions.)

5. REAL ESTATE:

(What will be done with the house, who will live there, who will be responsible for remaining mortgage payments, repairs, what special arrangements, if any, will be made for purchasing or renting any additional housing, and so on.)

6. PENSIONS AND SAVINGS:

(How any pension benefits will be paid out, how savings accumulated to date will be divided, if at all; all such matters to be determined by considering who will need what.)

7. SHARED BELONGINGS:

(Who will need what in the way of a car, furniture, household equipment, and so on.)

8. FUTURE INCOMES:

(What adjustments will be in order in the event of inheritances, new employment, significant loss, and so on.)

9. ILLNESS OR OTHER UNPREDICTABLE TURN OF EVENTS:

(Under what circumstances adjustments to all the foregoing may need to be considered, such as serious or prolonged illness, and so on.)

10. DEBTS:

(How existing or future debts of either party will be dealt with.)

11. PERSONAL POSSESSIONS:

(What is to be done with things of value owned by both but of primary interest only to one, such as heirlooms, special collections, and so on.)

12. DIVORCE:

Each of us agrees that, if either of us should desire a legal divorce and final dissolution of our marriage, for whatever reason, then the other will not contest such action or refuse to sign whatever document may be required to give swift effect to such action or raise any kind of obstacle whatever.

13. MEDIATION:

Each of us agrees not to seek the aid of any attorney for the settlement of any disagreement that may arise in connection with any matter dealt with in this agreement, or to engage any attorney to assist either of us to gain any concession from the other, beyond what may be minimally required in order to formalize a divorce, but instead to submit any problem arising under this agreement to impartial mediation.

(Signature)   (Signature)

_____   _____

(Notarization)

Having both signed the agreement in the presence of a notary public, each should in addition *initial* each page.

Can you do it? Probably not. The degree of cooperation required for such a self-managed separation and divorce is without doubt beyond the capacities of most couples, the more so since the stakes are so high. Yet it is certainly worth doing if you can, because it is the only way that both parties can win, in the only sense of winning that counts. The matters agreed to are in some cases vague—for example, living arrangements for children—and many needs will change with time. For example, the children will get older, and their needs will change; incomes and fortunes will change, for better or worse, and again, adjustments will be in order. Such things are possible only if a spirit of cooperation prevails.

Moreover, even if you cannot entirely succeed in such self-managed divorce, you will nevertheless have *tried* a cooperative approach, and this is by itself invaluable, even if, ultimately, it does not succeed. By establishing some sort of rapport by such an approach, you will each be far less likely to be tempted to "do the other in," and you will at least have seen how far cooperation can go. There is even a safety valve: if the cooperative approach becomes stalled, then you will have agreed to resolve what differences remain through mediation, and, with this background already established, even if to a far from perfect degree, mediation is certain to be easier, both for you and for the mediator.

It will be worthwhile, in any case, to get the help of a mediator to have a look at your agreement, whether that mediator has had any part in it or not. Be sure to find one who will encourage the cooperative approach, rather than someone who simply acts as a surrogate for lawyers and who will therefore want to think in terms of entitlements. By having such a mediator take a final look at things, you may discover that there is a better way to achieve some end; for example, a way that will save on tax liability without compromising any overall goals.

Step five: As a last step, you will need an attorney to file the agreement with the court for incorporation into the divorce decree. This must be an attorney you both agree to, preferably one who is already known to you both, and with the understanding on his or her part that you are not seeking legal advice, but only what amounts to a clerical service.

Finally, let it be noted that, as a general philosophical and ethical principle, cooperation, even when not total, always succeeds better than competition, and it is very possible that, through such an approach, divorcing couples can gain something that in the past has seemed out of reach; namely, continuing *friendship*. This is always precious, and when it can be achieved between people who have loved each other, and who may have children that both love, then it is precious beyond measure. If you can rise to the demands of reason, then you have it in your power to prove false something that has for so long seemed a tragic certainty to attorneys involved in divorce litigation, that is, that nothing stirs so much bitterness as divorce. And the blessing of continued friendship, and the inherent dignity of cooperation, will be all yours.

additional
resources

THE ALTERNATIVES TO MARRIAGE PROJECT

This was begun by two unmarried graduates of Brown University and has attracted vast coverage in leading newspapers, magazines, and on the radio. Its purpose is to promote successful cohabitation, including same-sex couples, by exploring the problems that often arise in nonlegal, de facto marriage relationships. It provides a large literature on the subject, plus a comprehensive and highly readable book, *Unmarried to Each Other*, and can be contacted at P.O. Box 991010, Boston, MA 02199.

DIVORCE MEDIATION

Professional divorce mediation, as an alternative to litigation, began in the seventies and has resulted in a vast literature, mostly by mediators whose backgrounds are in law, social work, and psychology. Two outstanding books are *Getting Divorced without Ruining Your Life*, by Sam Margulies (Simon & Schuster, 2001), and *Choosing a Divorce Mediator*, by Diane Neuman (Henry Holt and Co., 1996).